30 Ways in 30 Days to Save Your Family

30 Ways
in 30 Days
to Save
Your Family

Rebecca Hagelin

Since 1947
REGNERY
PUBLISHING, INC.
An Eagle Publishing Company

Cataloging-in-Publication data on file with the Library of Congress

ISBN 978-1-59698-568-1

Published in the United States by
Regnery Publishing, Inc.
One Massachusetts Avenue, NW
Washington, DC 20001
www.regnery.com

Manufactured in the United States of America

10   9   8   7   6   5   4   3   2   1

Books are available in quantity for promotional or premium use. Write to Director of Special Sales, Regnery Publishing, Inc., One Massachusetts Avenue NW, Washington, DC 20001, for information on discounts and terms or call (202) 216-0600.

Contents

Foreword

Remember when you first laid eyes on your newborn baby? Remember how tiny and vulnerable he seemed; or how determined you were to always protect her? Most parents pray that their children will grow up to be strong, productive, and patriotic, with a robust moral sense.

But as soon as you bring your children into the world, others try to pry them from you. Crass marketers try to lure them into commercialism. "Experts," from doctors to teachers, try to replace your good values with theirs. When we in the media talk about the "culture wars" what we're really talking about is the battle for our kids' hearts and minds.

Now, thankfully, Rebecca Hagelin has brought the ammunition that all of us, as parents, have long needed. In her terrific new book,

30 Ways in 30 Days to Save Your Family, she's given us the perfect guide, the perfect handbook, to keep a toxic culture at bay while forging a closer, deeper, more meaningful relationship with our children.

I've known Rebecca for many years, and her knowledge about cultural issues, the media, and the pressures on today's kids is vast. She's also a loving, committed wife and mother, and a marketing wizard. Her writings and speeches have encouraged many parents and families over the years, including mine. But what marks her most is her undying faith in God, forgiveness, and the hope that each new day brings. Even though her message is a somber one, Rebecca's spirit is lighthearted and optimistic—and her book provides practical solutions that, if put into practice, will strengthen each member of your family as well as the unit as a whole.

30 Ways in 30 Days to Save Your Family breaks down common parenting problems into manageable pieces and provides practical solutions that any frazzled parent can easily put to use. It is designed for today's parent, for today's problems; I'm sure it will speak to you as it spoke to me.

This is the handbook I wish America had years ago. Reading it gave me hope—both as a father and as a concerned citizen. Read and use Rebecca's book, and you can become the parent you always wanted to be.

—Sean Hannity

Introduction

I came very close to not writing this book.

How could I—an imperfect mother with an imperfect record—have the moral authority to even suggest to other parents how to raise their kids?

Shortly after my first book, *Home Invasion: Protecting Your Family in a Culture That's Gone Stark Raving Mad* hit the bookstores, a very-high profile writer for whom I have great respect said, "Rebecca, I saw your book in the window of the bookstore. Wow. You have a lot of guts—you have kids that can still embarrass you. You're very brave—or very foolish—to write a book on parenting."

Her words stung more than she realized. Yes, I do have three children who are living testaments to all of the great successes—and great mistakes—I've made as a parent. And, yes, I have made many, many blunders. But I let that comment play over in my head one too many times, and soon I began to doubt whether I had *any* right to try to help *any* parent do *anything.* Despite the many moving letters from parents thanking me for the tips, in spite of the warm embraces I received from moms and dads, and even teens, who attended speeches I made across the country, the fear that I would be shamed as a flawed parent started building in my heart and mind. Why on earth would I write a second book?

Please understand, I have great kids. My doubts were not about them. Drew, Nick, and Kristin are precious blessings—and I so admire the young men and young lady they have become. At the writing of this book, they are 21, 19, and 16—all are old enough to know the difference between right and wrong, yet still young enough to make serious mistakes that could affect the rest of their lives. I pray every day that they will make the right decisions—but it's now pretty much up to them to make their own choices. However, I can tell you this one thing for certain: They have been taught "right" and "wrong"—the two oldest did not leave our home wondering, and my youngest will not either.

Truth is a powerful tool. As parents, we have the obligation to step up to the plate and share what we know to be true with our kids. Too many moms and dads seem to be so concerned with image or political correctness that they fail to teach their kids what is noble, just, pure, and true. And I believe we have an obligation to help each other out, too. We parents aren't looking for the "perfect mom" or "perfect dad" to emulate—we are looking for help, validation, and formulas that have worked for others. I have been blessed with a unique opportunity to share what I have learned with moms and dads who don't want to miss the obvious or make mistakes just because they didn't know any better. I now believe that to be silent about what I have learned, about what I know to be true, would be immoral—something akin to a pediatrician withholding a medicine that he knows will help someone else's child—just because his own kids still get sick, too.

And I know there are plenty of parents who have wisdom to share, so in my column that is carried by Townhall.com, patriotpost.us, and other sites and papers across the country, I invited moms and dads to send me their own insights and tips on the thirty subjects I chose to write about. The e-mail came flooding in, and what you now hold in your hands is a work to which many of them contributed. In order to protect the privacy of people whose stories I share, I used only first names and in some cases, even changed those. I also edited some of the comments for clarity and brevity.

In addition to advice from other parents, I wanted input from my children—some assurance that what I wrote was authentic and actually works. So, I involved Drew, Nick and Kristin in the process. However, I will say up front—the inmates did not take over the asylum (a little joke there). And because they have never been parents—especially not parents of *themselves*—I didn't incorporate *all* of their changes or suggestions. I did, however, listen carefully, cry a few tears at the mistakes I made in raising them, and incorporated lessons learned from the school of hard knocks.

Drew and Nick gave pretty blunt feedback—and I thank them with all of my heart for it. We've always had a very close relationship, and I've loved every minute of being the mom of my two boys. Drew and Nick, I'm so proud of the young men you have become, and so very thankful that you have followed your passions and are pursuing the unique talents God has given each of you. Thanks for letting me hug on you endlessly throughout your childhood, and thank you for the ways you have shown your love to me.

When asked for specific points I should highlight, Drew, a pensive guy who is also blessed with a keen sense of humor and tons of creative talent, thought it was important for me to emphasize age-appropriateness in media consumption. In other words, to remind parents that movies or TV shows that might be unsuitable for seven-year-olds might be perfectly fine for fifteen-year-olds. He also said that he always believed my husband (Andy) and I didn't let him watch most R-rated flicks because we thought they would turn him into a bad person. My goodness—I discovered that I had failed miserably in explaining to our children that the main reason we are selective in our media choices is because much of the content is just plain raunchy. Andy and I decided long ago that media content that violates our consciences and what we understand to be right, would not be viewed in our household. It was heart-breaking to realize I had never adequately made the point that content can be wrong on its face. I suddenly remembered a saying my mother often used that illustrates the point, "I don't know why they call X-rated movies 'adult movies'—they aren't right for adults either!"

Drew also underscored something else—a critical insight that I hope you will take note of: the importance of being consistent in upholding the rules you have set. "When a parent isn't consistent, their 'rules' don't appear to have any meaning behind them. They also aren't even useful in trying to teach anything. When standards are inconsistently applied to some situations and not others, it also makes the parents look like they are discriminating against specific individuals."

Of course, he's right. Consistency is probably the toughest skill to master as a parent—and one of the most important. We can't disregard our own values and standards just because we're tired, not in the mood to fight, or lose our courage. And we can't "bend the rules" for some people when there is a value or principle at stake. When we do, it confuses the tender hearts and minds that have been put in our care.

Nick has a spunky, argumentative streak, an entrepreneurial spirit, and excels in design. As a child, he was always thinking past my next answer, and shared that it is important for parents to show a unified front on sensitive issues with their children. When my husband and I were firmly in agreement even Nick would give up trying to outwit us. Nick also wanted me to give parents a warning: your kids will get annoyed with you when you make and enforce rules that others aren't. However, he also said, "Now that I'm older I realize the importance of the standards and limits you set when we were kids." Wow. As a parent, that was very encouraging! Still, he also emphasized the importance of not having a lot of unnecessary and trivial rules. Both boys reflected on the tremendous impact it had on their behavior when we trusted them. For instance, my husband and I have never been huge believers in arbitrary curfews. We have always insisted on knowing where our kids were and with whom, and our ability to contact them via their cell phones whenever we want to. (By the way, as far as I'm concerned, the purpose of giving a child or teen a cell phone is so that mom and dad can call when they want to. That's always been a hard and fast rule with me—when I call, you best answer the phone or no more cell phone for you!) But we've never believed there was a magic bewitching hour they had to be home by. As long as they kept our trust and faith in them, they actually had more freedom than many of their peers. Drew summed up the impact that our faith in him had: "The fact that you and Dad thought we could handle ourselves and that I had your respect made me want to keep that respect. I definitely didn't want to violate the trust and do anything stupid. Knowing you trusted me helped me keep that trust. It's a much better system than having a bunch of meaningless rules."

Kristin, my sixteen-year-old daughter, helped me edit much of the book, and encouraged me to redraft several sections. A gifted writer and thoughtful young woman, Kristin was invaluable in keeping me motivated through very long days or when I was having difficulty expressing myself. She was inspiring and insightful throughout the process, and I've incorporated many of her ideas and stories in the book. Since she was still living under our roof when I was working hard to pull this together, she got called on a lot for instant feedback, editing help, and assistance! She also graciously wrote her own brief introduction—I was very moved (and amused) upon reading it. I hope you enjoy it, too.

Having your mom write a book about parenting is absolutely terrifying.

When my mom started working on her second book, I knew I wanted to be involved. I think she assumed I was helping her because writing is one of my passions and because, for me, getting my hands a little messy in the production of a book is tasting a little bit of bliss. Or maybe she thought I wanted to make sure that the ideas she was going to provide would make sense in the eyes of a teenager.

What I really wanted to do was save my name.

Sure, Mom said she wouldn't write anything that would embarrass me . . . but this just might be the one thing I will never fully trust her on. This was coming from the woman who thinks it's okay to tell my friends naked baby stories.

I was going to be sneaky. I had a plan. I told her I was going to check for typos and make little suggestions about the wording of things. And I did. But, secretly, I was also making sure nothing got said that I didn't want said.

I think she caught on. She has a way of doing that. It's like moms can read minds sometimes. I can't wait until I'm a mom and I can read minds . . . but that's beside the point.

The point is that as I was scanning the pages of her book, I realized why my mom is a superhero. (You can't blame me for being cheesy and saying things like she's a superhero. She says cheesy things, too, and I am her daughter. Besides, even when we say cheesy things, we mean them.) My mom is a superhero because her heart is in the right place, and because when she finds things that make her come alive, she goes and does

Introduction

them. The way I see it, the world has two problems. The first is that we all let our hearts get wrapped up in the wrong places and when we do, we forget about the things that really matter. The second problem is our fear, or timidity, or whatever it is that keeps us from chasing after the calling of our hearts once they are in the right place. My mom decided that the value of a strong family really matters to her, and she does everything in her power to preserve that value.

My world is a better place because she and my father dedicated themselves to providing my brothers and me with the best they could. They gave us everything we needed as kids, as maturing teenagers and young adults, as part of humanity, and as unique individuals. I believe the most important thing my parents gave us is their example. They showed us how to live, how to love, and what it means to have faith. I'm not sure if I could put to words why I believe their strong example has been so influential in my life, but one of my all-time favorite quotes does an amazing job of it. In his book, *Blue Like Jazz*, Donald Miller wrote, "I was outside the Baghdad Theater in Portland one night when I saw a man playing on the saxophone. I stood there for fifteen minutes, and he never opened his eyes. After that I liked jazz music. Sometimes you have to watch somebody love something before you can love it yourself." I have grown up witnessing undying love and persistent belief. They come easy for me because I have seen them at work. My parents would never have had to tell me what those words, love and faith meant, but they did that, too.

Art comes from the soul of the artist. It doesn't shy away from challenging culture, and it doesn't try to match the standards of society. Art represents what the artist is trying to convey, but it never reaches perfection. Parenting is a strange and *beautiful art form. I admire all parents who take up the role of the artist, who eagerly pursue their own potential and try to set an example for their children. I hope you will read this book and find inspiration, encouragement, technique, and an appreciation for the power of your own influence in the lives of your children.*

Chances are that even though I tried to prevent it, I'll turn a page in this book after it's published and blush. But I'm guessing I'll get over it pretty fast because it's really not that bad being embarrassed by a superhero.

And Mom, that's not an invitation.

Thanks, Girlfriend! You're a treasure.

I called for help from outside my family, too. Two great writers in very different life stages also helped me draft sections of the book and offered tremendous insights. One, Ashley Samelson, a young single woman, provided her perspective on the many pressures put on teens these days. Ashley is an amazing researcher and writer and has a brilliant future in whatever area she chooses. The second, Paul Gallagher, is a seasoned father of five and also an incredibly talented writer and editor. Paul and his wonderful wife, Cindy, have loads of insights to share on parenting—and their precious children are the result.

A very special thanks from the depths of my heart goes out to Rebekah Coons. "Bekah" kept me organized, on schedule, and helped me keep my sanity through many difficult days. She gave me the treasured gift of inspiration—one thing an author desperately needs when facing a looming deadline. She also shared a couple of very personal and moving stories on how her own parents influenced and shaped her life. I know you will enjoy them.

I also owe a huge debt of gratitude to my "small group"—the folks that Andy and I meet with nearly every Tuesday for Bible study and prayer. These dear friends prayed me through a lot of difficult times while I was writing the book, and I will always be thankful to them for their friendship, spiritual guidance and encouragement.

And, finally, to my dear hubby, Andy—thank you from the depths of my soul for being such an honorable father to our children. You will always be my Knight in Shining Armor and my "help meet." I pray that our children will one day have a marriage like ours—and I thank you for your undying loyalty, love, and friendship.

Commit To
The Daily Battle

THE CHALLENGE

Fighting the modern culture on a daily basis is tough. Today's families are busier than ever and it's so easy when you are tired or just plain worn out to throw in the towel and set your values aside. I know. I've been guilty of doing it myself sometimes. As a mother of three, I've had plenty of battles and challenges along the way. And I'm the first to admit that I've failed far too many times to uphold the standards I've said I believe in.

As parents, too many of us are so fearful of losing that we never try; others give in or give up along the way. Many parents don't seem to realize that in today's world, you must fight to protect your child's innocence, their childhood, their character—and their best futures. But it's a battle that's well-worth fighting.

According to the Institute for American Values' Motherhood Project, "Ninety-five percent [of mothers] wish American culture made it easier to instill positive values in children. Over eighty percent of mothers expressed concern about the influence of advertisements on children and, more generally, the influence of media. Over eighty-five percent of mothers also agree with the statement 'money has too much control over our lives' and agree that childhood should be a time when children are protected from large parts of the adult world." So the question is, why aren't these same moms doing more to protect their own sons and daughters?

Of course, such concern over the pop culture's negative influence on our kids is nothing new. One of the key motivators for my writing *Home Invasion* and this book in the first place was the thousands of e-mails I have received over the years from parents who read my column. They express frustration, anger, and often helplessness—all powerful emotions that come from the constant onslaught of what has become a culture that has gone stark raving mad.

We can't waste a single day. We have a very, very short time to mold our children's hearts, and to develop their minds and thinking. Each day that we fail to take the opportunities to forgive and discipline and teach lessons from the "school of hard knocks" is probably a day we will regret. Somewhere down the line our children are going to learn about consequences—some of which will be quite severe and suffered needlessly because we didn't teach them about the results of their actions when we had the chance.

For those of you who haven't yet started, or who perhaps have failed to live up to your own standards, I offer a word of truth and encouragement. You can start today—and you can still win.

If you have only recently come to the realization that your kids need you in the battle with them, please don't despair over the days lost. You must remember that despair is not an option. Beating yourself up endlessly over past mistakes can rob you of the incredible beauty and opportunity of today. Yes, your challenges might be greater, but each new day offers a chance to start over again. I've heard it said that "Parenthood is not a dress rehearsal—you get one chance to do it right." Although I believe that fully, it is equally important to remember that each morning offers a brand new chance to reclaim your home, to touch your child's heart in a deep and meaningful way, and to teach lessons that will always guide them.

You might not be able to save the world, although it is a noble and worthwhile effort to try your best to influence the overall culture for the better. But you can—you must—save your family. It doesn't take an act of Congress to make your home the nurturing environment it was intended to be. It does take developing a loving relationship with your children, a commitment to the daily battle, and making and upholding a pledge to become more involved in your kids' daily lives.

We've got to teach our children sound values at home so that when they are confronted with damaging messages outside the home, they can recognize them as such and know how to reject them. It's also imperative that we teach our children that our battle is not with them, but with other adults who have a different world-view and care nothing about their futures.

Let's be clear: Adults create and operate the hard-core porn sites; adults own the record companies that produce sexist, racist, and violent music; adults are the ones spamming your child's e-mail account with porn; adults are the ones designing and selling thongs to ten-year-olds; adults are the ones who allow the popular sites that kids visit like MySpace and YouTube to be filled with obscene material; and adults are spending billions of dollars on over-sexualized marketing campaigns aimed at your kids.

As I've said before, the problem isn't with "these kids today," the problem is with these adults today.

We must teach our kids character and values found in principles of courage, how to say "no," and how to rise and tower above the pop culture that seeks to do them harm. Moms and dads, if you don't stand in the gap for your kids, nobody is going to.

I'm not talking about building walls around your children that shut them off from the rest of the world. I'm talking about building within your children strength of character so that they will know how to make the right decisions when they go out the door every day into a world of temptation.

Days build upon days. They become weeks, and months, and years. And before you know it, your child is walking down the graduation aisle and out your door. When that time comes, you will be grateful for every moment you spent with your sons and daughters. As a mom with two boys in college and a daughter in high school, I will absolutely testify that you will relish every second you spent with them. And you will be so very thankful that you awoke each day with a heart purposed toward your child and his upbringing. You will never, ever regret the time you spend with your children, but you will mourn the days you missed. Vow to be engaged, every day, with your child. It is a vow that will serve you—and them—well.

IN YOUR SHOES

I wake every single morning with a prayer to my Lord asking for strength and a commitment to uphold the values that my husband and I have set for my household. My prayer goes something like this, "Dear God, please help me today—on this one day—to be the Mom you have called me to be. To be brave for my children; to be discerning, loving, gentle, and firm. And to always remember that you are only a prayer away."

It seems that just when I start to get discouraged or give up, God gives me a little reminder that I'm doing ok—one of my children, or even their friends, will say or do something that reminds me they appreciate and even value the tone we have set in our household.

One night, a few years ago, we had about six or seven teenage boys hanging out at our home, as usual. My husband and I make a point to create an atmosphere that reflects our belief that every child is special and welcome, and we have come to truly love and value the children around us. We often stay up very late with them on weekends, just talking. At around 2:00 a.m. (yes, that's 2:00 in the morning), one of the guys, Richard, said out of the blue, "Hey guys, I feel so at home here. Isn't it wonderful how we can go to each other's houses and all feel like we are with our own families?"

I share my story because committing to the daily battle isn't about being confrontational all the time. It's about up-holding standards and morality in such a way that all of the children who come into your home feel as if they are truly loved—as if they are part of a family that cares about them enough to challenge the status quo. If you have the right attitude and demeanor about enforcing rules of civility and respect and morality in your home, the tone of your home will be one of comfort. The environment of your home will be safe. And your kids and their friends will want to "hang out" there.

FROM MY HOME TO YOURS

Since I've asked you to fight the culture war every single day, it would probably be decent of me to offer a few practical tools for your arsenal.

❏ Physically love your child every day. (Read more about this in the section, "Teach Your Children Every Day That They Have God-Given Value.")

❏ When you take something away, replace it with something better.

❏ Respect your child's maturity—in other words, understand and consider what "age appropriate" material is. A movie that should be forbidden for your ten-year-old might be perfectly acceptable for your sixteen-year-old.

❏ Never expect that you have to "go it alone" in the battle. But at the same time, be prepared to do so. (In other words, look for allies in the battle, but don't stop doing the right thing in times when you find you are the only one that feels something is not right for your child.)

❏ Set time, as well as content limits, on media. Remember, it's the quantity of media our kids are consuming as well as the poor quality of the material that is hurting them.

❏ Spend as much time as possible actually engaging your children in conversation.

❏ Laugh. A lot. Default to laughter when possible.

❏ When tears flow from the eyes of your child, always wipe them away. Do so with a tender touch and humility.

❏ Never, ever, storm from the room angry. Remember, you are the adult—it is your responsibility to act like one.

❏ If your teenager storms from your presence into their bedroom, give them a while to calm down, and then gently knock on the door and insist on talking. But never, ever let the sun go down on their, or your, wrath. And never let an angry teen leave the home—especially if they are driving.

Commit to the Daily Battle

- ❏ When you mess up, miss the mark, or make an error in judgment, always apologize to your kids and ask their forgiveness.
- ❏ When your kids mess up and say they are sorry, never withhold your forgiveness and grace. Remember, they are learning about God's grace and mercy by watching you.
- ❏ Set content standards for your home and stick with them—no matter how tired you are.
- ❏ Watch television and movies with your child. When objectionable material comes up, discuss it with them. Remember, you aren't trying to shield them from everything—your goal should be to help them to develop discernment and judgment in gradual increments so that they can go out on their own and make moral and healthy decisions.

You'll find plenty of other helpful tips to help you in the daily battle in the section, "Make Your Home Inviting, Warm, And ... Fun!"

ACT NOW

Date _____

Today I pledge that every day from now on I will fight for my children and their futures. I will not back down. I will not grow so weary that I give up. And I will remember that, above all else, my goal is to show my children that I love them enough to dare to challenge the status quo.

_____
Signature

MORE HELP

■ At the fantastic site, passingthebaton.org, you can join others in receiving in-depth training on how to influence not only your kids, but their entire generation to be the next great leaders. Jeff Meyers, president of Passing The Baton has written a great book called, *Handoff: The Only Way to Win the Race of Life*. It is a "clarion call to enjoin what may be the most significant battle of our age—to mentor, coach and disciple the next generation of leaders." By 2015, the organization hopes to have mobilized one million adults to pass the baton of culture-shaping leadership to the next generation. I hope you will be one of them.

■ Read Sean Hannity's great book, *Let Freedom Ring: Winning the War of Liberty over Liberalism*. It examines being prepared to teach our children the fundamental principles and values that make our country great in light of the unique challenges we currently face.

Envision The Childhood
You Want For Your Children,
And The Adults You Want
Them To Become

THE CHALLENGE

As I travel the country speaking to civic, religious, and parenting organizations about the joys and challenges of parenting, I'm met with nearly universal desperation from parents who are sick and tired of always having to battle for their kids' hearts, minds, and very souls.

As the mother of three, I admit that I sometimes fall back in my own war with the culture. It's tough, tiresome, and even tedious. I sometimes forget exactly what it is I am trying to achieve. The trouble is, when caught up in the "tyranny of the urgent" and with the numerous struggles of each day, losing sight of the big picture is very easy.

The Good Book says, *"Without a vision, the people perish."* I submit to you that perhaps the biggest reason that so many of our families and children seem to have lost their way is that we, as a culture and as individuals, have lost sight of the vision of the lives we want for our children.

Some parents have been so overwhelmed since the day that tiny bundle was placed in their arms that they have never really stopped to consider the childhood they want their offspring to *have*—or the adult that child should *become*.

But whether liberal, conservative, or somewhere in-between, I'm convinced that all decent parents pretty much want the same thing for their kids. We want them to be happy and safe, and develop into adults of character. Taking the time to picture what childhood should be like helps us protect it. And creating a vision of our children's best future reminds us of the prize. It's not enough for us to be *against* things, we must be *for* something, too. We must know what we believe and be purposeful about making it a reality. It helps to actually write it down—here's what I wrote:

> *I believe that childhood should occur within a protected space of innocence. I believe that our children should be able to daydream and play in their "make believe" world, far from "adult" concerns and adult issues. I believe that our daughters should be free from the fear of pregnancy, and that our sons should not have to worry about sexually transmitted diseases. I believe that my children should also be free from teenage sexual activity and the complexities and guilt that come when their innocence is compromised. I believe that our kids should know there is a Creator who loves them and has a unique purpose for their lives. I believe they should understand that we are here for them—that mom and dad are committed to answering their questions, challenging their intellect, and that they can depend on us to guide them. I believe that our children should feel confident enough in our*

gentleness to come to us with their own hopes, dreams, and fears. I believe that the teenage years should be filled with conversations, laughter, and a warm and secure place called "home." I also want my children to grow up and have happy families of their own. I want them to be marked by good character and generosity; to be responsible, honest, healthy, and courageous; to be respected and respectful; to live their dreams with no encumbrances from mistakes made in their youth; to know what it's like to be committed to someone fully—and to understand the value and honor in being loyal, true, and just.

Have you ever deliberately thought about the type of adults you want your children to become? What do you believe childhood and the teen years should look like? I'm not asking what they *do* look like—but what they *should* look like. Now write it down. (It doesn't have to be deeply profound or complicated. Feel free to borrow from my vision statement, or from your own childhood experiences growing up. What did you long for? What did your parents do right?)

_____

_____

_____

_____

_____

_____

_____

There's not one parent reading this book that actually wants his son to grow up to be a lazy bum. There's not one dad who wants his daughter to be known as a slut; not one mother who is hoping her child will go through multiple marriages that end in painful divorce. None of us want our children to get sexually transmitted diseases, have abortions, or end up addicted to drugs.

What are we doing now to prepare our children to become the adults we envision? And, of course, the follow-up question is, "What are we doing to create that reality?" We must constantly remember the beautiful, lovely, fulfilling lives we want our kids to enjoy, and start understanding that the decisions we make today about how we raise them will have a direct impact on how they choose to live their lives when they are on their own.

IN YOUR SHOES

I think one of the greatest visionaries of our time was the late Martin Luther King, Jr. He ignited an entire nation and helped bring liberty to an oppressed people, while changing the course of history—all by being committed to a vision. He is an example of how articulating a dream can help make it a reality. His incredibly moving speech said, in part:

I have a dream that one day this nation will rise up and live out the true meaning of its creed: "We hold these truths to be self-evident, that all men are created equal."

I have a dream that one day on the red hills of Georgia, the sons of former slaves and the sons of former slave owners will be able to sit down together at the table of brotherhood.

I have a dream that one day even the state of Mississippi, a state sweltering with the heat of injustice, sweltering with the heat of oppression, will be transformed into an oasis of freedom and justice.

I have a dream that my four little children will one day live in a nation where they will not be judged by the color of their skin but by the content of their character.

Dr. King's dream was for his children and all of the children that would follow after them. He held on to his vision and never let go. Because he could visualize it, he could articulate it—which he did time and time again. And because he could articulate it, he was able to inspire others to visualize the dream, and to work against all odds to achieve it.

I believe that we, as parents, can do that too.

Our personal battle may not be against racism or sexism or the oppression of a people. But it is a battle all the same—against the forces that would oppress traditional values, decency, and honor. It is a battle against a world that treats our children as something less than human. Dr. King spoke not just of ending racial inequality, but of creating a world where children would be judged only by the "content of their character." That should be the dream we also have for our children.

FROM MY HOME TO YOURS

Of course the very idea of having a specific vision that you constantly keep in the front of your mind is timeless, and has been proven over and over again to work. One of the best-selling books of the modern age is Norman Vincent Peale's *The Power of Positive Thinking*, in which he describes how our thinking shapes who we become. But long before Dr. Peale, there was the wisdom of the Bible. One of the most powerful scripture verses is Proverbs 23:7, *"As a man thinketh in his heart, so is he."* Children and teens usually end up being exactly who they think they are, which is often a result of who the adults around them think they will be. It's not enough for us to have a vision; we must teach our children to have one, too—and to think about it every day.

We must teach them to understand that, regardless of their circumstances, they have total control over their character and actions toward others. Talk about personal power! We have to remind them (and ourselves) that although they might not be able to control what happens to them, they are in complete control of how they react to the events of their daily lives.

Giving our children the gift of positive thinking is priceless and will serve to actually help them shape their behavior into a positive force. If they start off every morning thinking about the things they are thankful for, the things they wish to be, and how they must advance what is good, the chances are very high that their actions will support their thought processes.

One of the very best resources I know to help us and our children focus on the way things should be, rather than getting bogged down with the negative, is Tommy Newberry's *New York Times* Bestseller, *The 4:8 Principle*. The focus of Tommy's book is Philippians 4:8, which reminds us how to add a bounce to our step and honor to our lives. The verse teaches us to think about truth, honor, justice, purity, loveliness, and good news. It tells us that if we train ourselves to think about these positive things, we will actually feel better and our lives and actions will begin to reflect those virtues. The verse says, "Finally, brethren, whatsoever things are true, whatsoever things are honorable, whatsoever things are just, whatsoever things are pure, whatsoever things are lovely, whatsoever things are of good report; if there be any virtue, and if there be any praise, think on these things."

As Newberry explains, *"Research indicates that the average person thinks approximately 50,000 thoughts per day, and each thought either moves us toward our full potential, or away from it. Unfortunately, we live in a society bent on nursing old wounds and high-*

lighting what is wrong with just about everything and everyone. As a result, we have grown accustomed to viewing the world, our lives, and ourselves through a lens of negativity—and that negativity stands in direct contrast to the positive, passionate, and purpose-filled people God wants us to be."

I often wonder how different our world would be if the precious minds of all of America's teens were filled with thoughts of truth, honor, justice, purity, beauty, and good news—I'm guessing that it would transform our culture overnight! Teaching your child to think this way could make his teen years far more beautiful than what the pop culture can give him. And teaching her to think positively now will result in the likelihood that she will carry those thoughts with her for the rest of her life.

Not long ago I had the amazing opportunity to hear Tommy Newberry speak—and my very special guest at the event was my then fifteen-year-old daughter, Kristin. She sat in such rapt attention to his message that it surprised even me. Her heart seemed to absorb every word like a sponge. She made sure we picked up a copy of his book, and I later found it in her room with passages marked by her own hand. It wasn't until then that I fully realized just how hungry our kids are for positive messages—or just how much negative garbage is forced into their brains by the pop culture. Even in my home, my own daughter was starving for solid advice on how to fight the clutter of negative messages being forced upon her by our culture.

I'm also thankful to report that Kristin's captivation by such a life-giving message was not short-lived. Recently, after I had a particularly bad day, I was griping and complaining in short bursts throughout the evening. My comments weren't directed at anyone in particular, but it was apparently pretty obvious that I was in a very negative state of mind. I just couldn't let go of the injustices of the day, thus allowing the bad day to create a less than joyful atmosphere for my family. After a while, Kristin had had enough. She very gently, and very respectfully said, "Mom, do you remember the 4:8 principle?" Such an abrupt reminder of truth from my teen daughter was just what I needed. I laughed, told her she was right, and in that very moment decided to forbid my brain from replaying the "horrors" of the day. I determined that I would instead think about all the wonderful blessings in my life. That doesn't mean I didn't continue to create a plan on how to correct the mistakes and deal with the consequences of the day—it meant that I decided to enjoy what was good, and came up with a positive plan on how to move the bad into a better direction. Rather than dwelling on the injustices, I switched to a mode of focusing on how I could create justice; instead of reliving wrongs done to me, I started focusing on forgiveness and thanking God for all the times I had experienced grace and mercy; instead of worrying about the consequences I would suffer from the results of someone else's error, I started coming up with solutions. In that moment, like never before, I realized how critical it is to not let someone else steal our happiness. And I learned that when we take the time to teach our children the value of holding on to a vision of loveliness, it just might circle back to help us hold on to our own dreams, too.

ACT NOW

Date _____

Today I wrote down the vision I have for my children and for their futures. I also sat down and shared that vision with them, and listened to their feedback.

_____
Signature

Envision the Childhood You Want For Your Children...

Assess Your Home

THE CHALLENGE

Most parents just don't know the content of the media their children are consuming on a daily basis. But once you have determined the vision you have for your child and his future, you must take inventory of his daily life to determine if the messages he is consuming support—or work against—the vision you have for his life. According to a recent Kaiser Family Foundation report, today's teens consume $6^1/_2$ hours to $8^1/_2$ hours of media each day due to multi-tasking (such as listening to their iPods while they surf the internet or playing a video game while they watch television). Most parent don't know that the number-one cable program teen girls choose is the racy MTV; that the number-one music genre choice for kids from all races and socio-economic levels is the often foul rap and hip hop; or that 90 percent of kids who go online stumble across hard-core porn, simply because parents have never taken the time to install a filter.

It's time for a little opposition research.

We must spend some time in their world, to find out which messages are being pumped into our children's still-developing brains, and how much pressure they are under from manipulative marketers trying to get a piece of the 200 billion dollars that America's teens spend each year. Today's children have more disposable income than any other generation of kids in history. And greedy companies know it. They will do anything to get your kids hooked on the adrenaline high that comes with viewing sexualized and violent media, and to spend money in pursuit of it.

The mass marketers are after your children 24/7. They slam your kids' e-mail inbox with pornography. They prominently display products and a life-style of betrayal, moral relativism, and sex, sex, sex in television programs. They are never too busy or too tired from a long day's work to pay attention to your child. They know how to get our teens to spend money: Feed their raging hormones and emotional roller coasters with adrenaline-pumping, non-stop messages of sex, violence, and rebellion. (More on this in the next chapter, Understand How Marketers Target Your Children.)

The reality is most parents don't want to look or listen too closely to what their kids are doing. Why? Because if we find objectionable media habits, then we're faced with having to do something about them—or turn our backs on the problem and our kids. For many parents, it's just easier to remain ignorant. We often choose peace over principle. We value a quiet home with uneasy smiles more than we value developing our children's character, risking possible conflict along the way.

The ugly truth is that in many cases, the American home has become a septic tank for the culture's toxic sewage. After all, teens at school may share the Web addresses for pornographic sites, or dish about the wildest sex scenes on television, or recommend the latest violent video game, but it's often in the privacy of their own bedrooms that our sons and daughters consume hour upon hour of the sludge that is perverting their views of sexuality, relationships, and life in general. It's time for us as moms and dads to pay attention to what's going on in our daughters' and sons' bedrooms, and in our own family rooms. Children are like blank slates when they are handed to us as newborn babies. Their minds are ready to be filled with good things or with bad things and it's up to moms and dads to provide a healthy mental diet. I've heard it said, "Garbage in—garbage out." Our children will largely become what they consume. It's up to us to provide them with the materials that will build courage, fortitude, fidelity, sound judgment, and strong character. But if you have no idea what others are pumping into their developing minds, how on Earth are you going to protect them? How are you going to select age-appropriate materials and teach them how to decipher negative images if you don't know what they are? Moms and dads, if you don't stand in the gap for your kids, nobody is going to.

FROM MY HOME TO YOURS

- As I mentioned, the number-one television viewing choice of teenage girls is MTV. The Medical Institute in Austin, Texas has analyzed music videos and found that 60–70 percent of them contain highly sexualized material. And of that, a full 81 percent connect violence to sex every single time.
- According to the Kaiser Family Foundation's report on media usage, "Children's bedrooms have increasingly become multi-media centers, raising important issues about

supervision and exposure to unlimited content. Two-thirds of all 8–18-year-olds have a TV, while half have a video game system in their bedrooms. Increasing numbers have a VCR or DVD player, cable or satellite TV, computer, and Internet access in their bedroom. Those with a TV in their room spend almost $1^1/_2$ hours more in a typical day watching TV than those without a set in their room. Outside of their bedrooms, in many young people's homes, the TV is a constant companion: nearly two-thirds say the TV is 'usually' on during meals, and half say they live in homes where the TV is left on 'most' or 'all' of the time, whether anyone is watching it or not."

■ Even while many polls show that parents are concerned about what their children watch and learn from the media, according to the Kaiser report, "About half of all 8–18-year-olds say their families have no rules about TV watching. Forty-six percent say they do have rules, but just 20 percent say their rules are enforced 'most' of the time. The study indicates that parents who impose rules and enforce them do influence the amount of time their children devote to media. Kids with TV rules that are enforced most of the time report two hours less daily media exposure than those from homes without rules."

In order to understand her world, walk one week in your child's tennis shoes. What is she listening to, watching, and reading? Take a trip to the mall and look at the posters that scream out to her from the music and clothing stores—what do the images portray? Anorexic-looking teen girls and young women in skimpy underwear adorn the windows of many clothing stores. When my daughter and I pass by such windows in lingerie stores, I don't ignore them—I take the time to point out how sad it is that young women would lower themselves to appearing shamelessly in their underwear in order to gain fame and fortune.

Music has long been the language of romance. Some of the most moving and inspirational songs of all time are about love and the mystery of the male–female attraction. But what the modern culture has done to this romance language in many cases is distort and cheapen it. Listen to your kids' iPods. Make a point to scroll through their menu of songs and take inventory of the often foul and disrespectful lyrics that stream directly into their brains. Put the earplugs into your head like your son does, feel the emotional beat and sensuality of the music like your daughter feels it, and listen to the words and messages. My guess is that in many cases, your heart will break over what you have discovered. It may be a rude awakening, and you may want to hang your head in despair over the lost innocence of your child.

Have you ever actually sat down and played one of your son's video or online games? You might be more than shocked to find out the content of best-selling games like the *Grand Theft Auto*™ series. As the title suggests, the goal is to steal cars. If that's all there was to it, it would be bad enough, but it gets worse: in the game, the way to acquire and hold on to the cars is to kill the police officers who try to stop you. And the sick minds behind the game give you plenty of choices—shooting them with a rifle, cutting them up with a chainsaw, setting them on fire, or decapitating them. If you shoot an officer, you get extra points for shooting him in the head. In another game that was popular a few years ago, the player could stuff dollar bills into the panties of dancing showgirls. Is that really what you want your son to be "virtually" doing in the privacy of your own home? Thousands of kids engage their imaginations, eyes, and minds in these and other violent and sexual activities via the big screen while good moms and dads are just a room or two away—blissful in their ignorance.

Video games simply aren't in the same class as movies and TV when it comes to making an impression on young minds. The latter offers a passive experience; you watch other people doing things. But with video games, your child becomes a participant. Your son actually becomes the character that rapes the girl, decapitates the police officer, and beats the prostitute. Your son decides who lives—and who dies. He alone pulls the trigger with the click of the controller he holds in his hand.

According to Dr. Elizabeth Carll of the American Psychological Association, this active participation enhances the "learning" experience. And, unlike a movie or a TV show that might be viewed once or twice, the games are played repeatedly, often for hours on end.

IN YOUR SHOES

I recently received an e-mail from Debbie, who shares these thoughts:

Watch TV with your kids! I don't necessarily approve of all of the shows, but my daughter's peer group does and by watching them, I learn the perspective of their age group and can point out the fallacies of these programs. The Internet is another tough one. The computer geeks at work gave me a program link that allows me to spy on my daughter's MySpace. I was pleasantly surprised. She lists me and her 9-year-old brother among her heroes (her dad gets strokes too). Other parents have not had such pleasant experiences. But you have to know what your kids are doing and that's one way to do it. My daughter gives me the password to her email accounts. I have read some tortured and profane emails from her friends and I have seen her replies and I'm proud of her. She is a role model to her peer group. But that didn't happen by accident.

Assess Your Home

She knows I'm looking over her shoulder and I think maybe she's more careful about her replies because somebody might read them.

What kind of influence are you having on your kids at home? Has your home merely become the pit stop where people sleep, keep their clothes, bathe, and have the occasional meal together? Or, is it something more? How you view your home is essential to how effective and nurturing your home will or will not be for your children. Have you ever really thought about it?

ACT NOW

Date _____

    Today I started taking inventory of my home. I told my kids that I care enough about them to start watching, listening to, and reading what other adults are telling them. I vow to go through my home and analyze the content of what I find in light of the vision I have set for my children. And I vow to never again be ignorant of the pressures placed on my kids by the mass media.

_____

Signature

I evaluated my child's:

❏ video games _____

_____

(list of games) on _____(date).

❏ TV shows_____

_____

(list of shows) on _____(date).

❏ e-mail/Facebook/MySpace accounts _____

_____

(list of accounts) on _____ (date).

Understand How Marketers Target Your Children

THE CHALLENGE

As I mentioned in the previous chapter, today's kids are the most marketed-to generation in history. They spend an estimated $200 billion a year of their own money so they are very profitable targets for exploitation and manipulation. Combine this with the frequently manifested modern parental desire to be their children's friend, and you can see why marketers compete like never before for the attention of these sophomoric spenders.

So fierce is the competition for their cash that modern marketing techniques have become, in many cases, insidiously evil. Selling to tweens isn't about finding out what they want—it's about figuring out how to manipulate their minds.

Sex sells, and is a staple of today's marketing campaigns. However, many of the highly sexualized campaigns today are targeted at children. They sell empty promises of sexual power, every kind of sexual perversion, and a crude incivility in entertainment programming, as well as specific products.

MTV (with its "pooh cam"—which enabled one to watch others go to the bathroom—and its tawdry Spring Break specials) and others have become experts at feeding the raging hormones, edginess, and roller-coaster emotions of our youth, producing highly titillating material that ignites their adrenaline and leaves them begging for more. Instead of helping our sons and daughters positively approach and channel their sexuality and their developing understanding of decency and civility, the entertainment world pours gasoline on youthful passions and confusion.

Plainly put, our kids are being used.

To understand why—and how—marketers target them, consider these facts, courtesy of the Campaign for a Commercial-Free Childhood:

- Children under 14 spend about $40 billion annually. Compare this to the $6.1 billion those between the ages of 4–12 spent in 1989. Teens spend about $159 billion.
- Children under 12 influence $500 billion in purchases per year.
- This generation of children is the most brand-conscious ever. Teens between 13 and 17 have 145 conversations about brands per week, about twice as many as adults.
- Companies spend about $17 billion annually marketing to children, a staggering increase from the $100 million spent in 1983.
- Children ages 2–11 see more than 25,000 advertisements a year on TV alone, a figure that does not include product placement (showing a character drinking a Coke, for ex-

ample). They are also targeted with advertising on the Internet, cell phones, mp3 players, video games, school buses, and in school.

- Almost every major media program for children has a line of licensed merchandise including food, toys, clothing, and accessories. Brand-licensed toys accounted for $22.3 billion in 2006.
- In their effort to establish cradle-to-grave brand loyalty and promote nagging, marketers even target babies through licensed toys and accessories featuring media characters.
- Viral marketing techniques take advantage of children's friendships by encouraging them to promote products to their peers.

As the National Institute on Media and the Family notes, when it comes to marketing to kids, the old equation has been turned on its head. Years ago, marketers would reach out to parents to get the kids. Today, they can go directly to the kids. Of course, that makes their job easier because children are certainly less discriminating and skeptical than adults, and therefore easier to persuade. As the cliché goes, "follow the money." That's exactly what marketers have done—and the easiest path is the one through your child's pocket.

What makes this all the more disturbing is the *content* of their messages. At best, marketers breed a highly materialistic view of life, leading kids to believe that happiness can be found in a line of stylish new clothes, the latest "hot" music, or an exciting new toy. But as the luster fades with the most recent acquisition, the desire for another new thrill takes its place. The temptation to be up-to-date with friends and classmates induces many kids (and many willing parents) to live beyond their means, trapping themselves in a spiritually empty cycle of "buy now, pay later" as they frantically try to keep up with the latest and greatest.

Worse is the trashy content in many ads and TV shows. To appear to be cutting edge, companies apparently see no choice but to lower standards, and to feed us crass images of sexuality and rebellion. As an executive from the WB network told PBS, "Teens are consumed with sex. It's all around them. If you're going to reach them, you have to talk about it."

This is so lazy. Take it from the mother of two sons: boys aren't "consumed" with sex. With girls? Sure. But being crazy about girls and "consumed" with sex are different things. Maybe if images of sex weren't "all around them," thanks to the WB and others, more boys would think about girls as human beings instead of just sex objects. But that would be hard, and selling sex is easy.

These companies *do* work hard at one thing, though: marketing their tasteless products. They conduct focus groups, stop kids on the street, grill them about their interests, and photograph them. MTV executives even visit the homes of typical teen viewers to better understand their targets. And what's the result of all this? The creation of characters that MTV uses across their programming who feed the egos and worst instincts in our kids. Why? So they will keep tuning into the programming and be exposed to the commercials their advertisers pay for.

They also market their own worldview. As the PBS special, *The Merchants of Cool* explains, MTV has created caricatures of teen boys and girls known as "Mooks" and "Midriffs." The Mook is "wilder and bolder and ruder and cruder than the average boy; they are pro wrestlers, the stars of the Jackass TV show, and the guys on MTV's Spring Break specials dancing crazily with scantily clad women they met 10 minutes earlier." The Midriff is consumed with her sexual power. She uses her body and an attitude of superiority to control those around her. The marketing geniuses that make MTV the number one viewing choice for teenage girls know exactly what they are doing—manipulating girls to become manipulators themselves.

Understand How Marketers Target Your Children

Today's media has made an industry out of studying your kids. It's time to know what they know about your sons and daughters, and then teach your kids how not to become a pawn in the name of greed.

Learn about the forces arrayed against you and arm your kids with the truth. Read *The Marketing of Evil: How Radicals, Elitists, and Pseudo-Experts Sell Us Corruption Disguised As Freedom* by David Kupelian, the managing editor of WorldNetDaily.com Today's youth are under tremendous pressure to conform to the value system of those who are selling them short of the best they can become—but we can't protect them if we don't know how they are doing it.

And we've got to do more than just know it. We've got to teach our children about marketing techniques and instill sound values in their hearts along with the will to stand up against those who would use them. If we take the time and energy to equip our sons and daughters, then when they are confronted with damaging, clever marketing messages, they will recognize them and know how to reject them.

One way to counteract the effect of advertising is to help your kids dissect it. That's the advice of Bob Smithouser, an editor with Focus on the Family's *Plugged In Online* (pluggedinonline.com). "Are your young people savvy enough to spend wisely?" he writes:

Here are questions you can ask teens as you dissect advertising:

❏ What is the sponsor really selling, the product itself or just an image connected with the product?

❏ Is this ad trying to exploit a human weakness such as vanity, lust, greed, pride, envy, or a desperate need to be accepted by others?

❏ What's the catch? Is there fine print or a hidden disclaimer that exposes this as an offer that really is too good to be true?

❏ Why do some ads want customers to "buy now, pay later"? What will that cost in the long run?

❏   Do I really need this product, or is the sponsor just trying to create a need for this product? People are constantly being made to feel insecure about bad breath, impending baldness, or the devastation of a dropped cell phone call. And for every manufactured fear, there's a product or service waiting to restore calm.

❏   What information is conveniently left out of this commercial message? For example, beyond the sticker price, certain vehicles cost more to insure and maintain than basic transportation.

[C]ursing advertising or blaming it for leading us into temptation is pointless. Rather, we must arm ourselves and our teens with the tools to deconstruct ads and expose those with questionable agendas. Manipulative advertisers prey on people's insecurities. They encourage comparison ('Be like—or better than—the guy next door'), which destroys contentment.

Let's give our teens the perspective to see beyond commercial messages that get in the way of what's really important.

The good news is that, as the Kaiser Family Foundation has reported, kids say their parents have tremendous influence on them. When children and teens face problems or questions, they are more likely to go to Mom or Dad first for advice and help if the parent has previously taken the initiative to talk to and teach their children about difficult issues.

The question is, what kind of influence are you having on your children?

When you ignore or pretend you don't see unhealthy, immoral, or just plain tacky and cheap messages, your child interprets your silence as an endorsement of the material. When you mindlessly plunk down sixty bucks for the latest video game, or give your ten-year-old the cash to buy clothes that make her look like a street-walker, you're part of the problem.

Don't walk silently past that Victoria's Secret display at your local mall. Tell your kids why it's wrong. Ask your children pointed questions about the TV shows and movies that interest them. Find out what they think—so you can spark discussions that will give you a chance to tell them what *you* think—and why.

IN YOUR SHOES

I recently asked the readers of my regular column how they deal with advertising. Here is how one mom responded:

One of the best ways to fight materialism, sexualization, and lack of respect is...to limit the amount of time on the television. My husband and I work at this two ways. First of all, we established when they were young that the TV only goes on after they have been given permission, and we establish how long it's going to be on (each child got to choose one half-hour show a day—subject to our approval). We pushed PBS shows, even if we had to occasionally point out some things the people were saying that were mistaken, just because then we didn't have to deal with commercials. When they got old enough to see commercial TV, I used a technique I learned from my mother—I would watch with them, and point out, derisively if it seemed right, the sales pitch of the commercial. So when the commercial showed someone doing something awkwardly so that the 'Peel-o-Matic' could then be hawked, I could say, 'Boy, that lady doesn't know how to peel carrots, does she? You're better at peeling than she is.' After a while, the children start noticing the assumptions and tactics and commenting on them—and for a while, you'll have to live with their preaching back to you. But they become wary of commercials.

Another mom wrote:

I explain to my kids that advertising is paid space that companies, politicians, and others buy in order to get people to do something. Most of the advertising that my kids see is to get them to spend their money, or to bug me to spend mine! I am careful to explain that part of what makes a powerful ad is to build desire in someone—to make them want something so badly, that they will pick up the phone and spend money at that moment to buy it. We discuss commercials as they come on television and I ask, "What is that the company selling? How did the commercial make you feel?" And, "Did you feel that way before you saw or heard the ad?" I'm also very deliberate about explaining that television shows and movies try to sell things too—mostly ideas about how people should behave. They often tell stories in an emotional way so that the viewer (my son or daughter) will feel a connection and want to keep watching. Then I explain that the greater the number of people that watch the show, the more money the stations can charge for advertising—so it all comes back to how much money can be made. But I also point out there is nothing wrong with wholesome entertainment, commercials, or good story-telling—as long as you know that the person doing it has an agenda.

Understand How Marketers Target Your Children

MORE HELP

Here are four great websites for helping you figure out what marketers are trying to sell to your kids.

PARENTS TELEVISION COUNCIL (parentstv.org). This great organization's mission is "to promote and restore responsibility and decency to the entertainment industry in answer to America's demand for positive, family-oriented television programming." I constantly depend on ParentsTV.org for the latest information and action steps I can take to have an impact on what ends up being broadcast across the nation's airwaves. You can be involved in one of their local chapters or campaigns to directly contact advertisers who should not be spending their dollars to support programs that promote irresponsible or immoral behavior. The Parents Television Council should be one of the first groups you count on. And if you're looking to become involved in the battle, they will equip you well.

CAMPAIGN FOR A COMMERCIAL-FREE CHILDHOOD (commercialfreechildhood.org). Their slogan is "Reclaiming Childhood from Corporate Marketers." That's exactly what our goal as parents has to be, and the

continued

MORE HELP

CCFC works to make it a reality. They emphasize concrete action, as a look at their Oct. 20, 2008 homepage made clear: It carried articles about their successful drive to get Scholastic Inc. to stop hawking its dreadful, over-sexualized "Bratz" dolls in schools, a way for parents to get Burger King and other companies to stop marketing PG-13 rated movies like *The Dark Knight* and *The Incredible Hulk* to kids, and a petition to the FCC to ban "embedded" ads and other product placements in kids' TV shows.

NATIONAL INSTITUTE ON MEDIA AND THE FAMILY (mediafamily.org). You'll find lots of good information on this site. When you join, the Institute will send you its "Parent Survival Guide to Advertising." The site also contains guides to help you make sense of the various types of ratings that are out there, for everything from video games to TV shows. You'll find out more about how media affects brain development and your child's ability to study. The Institute also has a lot of basic information for those interested in learning more about marketing and kids. Want to know, for example, how television affects reading levels? Or what it does to girls' body image? The Institute has fact sheets for these and many other topics.

SALVO (salvomag.com): It's the best magazine out there on the insidious effects of marketing and the media. Salvo is "dedicated to debunking the cultural myths that have undercut human dignity, all but destroyed the notions of virtue and morality, and slowly eroded our appetite for transcendence." (I so appreciate the mission of Salvo that I volunteer my time as a senior editor.) It's perfect for young adults raised on the attention-grabbing graphics of today's Internet. And Salvo doesn't shy away from tough topics. The first issue, for example, tackled cloning, euthanasia, evolution, and eugenics. You can find out more, and order a sample copy, at salvomag.com.

Make Your Home Inviting, Warm, And...Fun!

THE CHALLENGE

When parents become aware of the cultural challenges, a common mistake is to go overboard and shut down all opportunities for fun. Although you must never compromise your values and principles, sticking to them doesn't mean turning your home into a lifeless, cold environment where your personal list of "Thou shalt nots!" is overwhelming. If you have an uninviting home, then neither your kids nor their friends will want to "hang out" there.

Children and teens are drawn to warmth, love, and excitement. But they also want to be in a nurturing environment where they feel safe and have boundaries. Your challenge is to create a home that provides all of these.

In a lecture at The Heritage Foundation in 2008, noted historian David Patterson encouraged people to think of the home as having the highest calling:

> Russell Kirk noted that 'cultural restoration, like charity, begins at home.' And he was quite right. For cultural restoration entails the restoration of what is most high, most dear, most enduring. And the ground for all such things is the home. The home is the place where our names are first uttered with love and therefore where we first discover that we mean something. It is the site where both human beings and human values first make their appearance in the world. It is the center from which we define and understand the nature of everything we encounter in the world. The home, then, is not one thing among many in a world of things; nor is it merely the product of a culture. Rather, the world of things derives its sense, and a culture its significance, from their relationship to the home. Without the home, everything else in the world or in a culture is meaningless.

Patterson continued:

> The home, then, might be better understood not as a place or a thing, but as an event in the life of the holy. Viewed as such an event, the emergence of the family that constitutes the home is far more than just a biological phenomenon or even a natural wonder. A mother, for example, is not just one who gives birth, but one who emanates light, love, and compassion. Through her, humanity receives a revelation of the light created upon the first utterance of Creation, the light that sanctifies all Creation.

Make Your Home Inviting, Warm, and...Fun!

It's pretty sobering to think about the fact that I, as a mother, am called to "emanate light, love, and compassion." I love my children completely and unconditionally. I would take a bullet for each of them. But the harsh reality is that my intense love does not always come across as, well, loving. I know that although I am moved with compassion for my children when they hurt, when they make mistakes, and when they have to suffer consequences, they often don't see or feel my compassion—sometimes they only see my anger, disappointment, and fear. And if these emotions manifest themselves into a mere list of do's and don'ts, then I—and my children—have missed the point of this special place called home.

It's time to understand the difference between a "house" and a "home," and vow to make yours one to come home to every day.

A house is a place where there are walls, floors, and rooms. It is a physical structure of function and utility. It is cement and pipes and wood and wiring, all void of human understanding, emotion, and creativity. It is governed by the parameters of the physical world—the water comes out *here,* you can access electricity *there;* paint peels, wood rots, and weeds eventually take over.

A home, on the other hand, is a place of belonging, acceptance, and comfort. It is a place where family members can make mistakes, be challenged to be their best, and experience the warmth that comes with grace, forgiveness, and redemption. It is where our life stories are molded, where verses and chapters are added as the years pass. It is a space for the development of the soul, the shaping of the spirit, and the expansion of the mind. A home is a place for reflection and quiet and solitude—a respite from the pressures of the world. And I believe that a home should also be a place of laughter, warm memories, and zany fun.

There is much in this book on the importance of establishing rules and boundaries for your home. Right now, I would like to focus on how to make it inviting.

FROM MY HOME TO YOURS

Don't make your house a "NO!" Zone. I've done literally thousands of radio interviews around the country on the issue of protecting our homes and families from an ever-invading crude culture. Invariably, at least one well-meaning caller will say something like, "I agree that the culture is evil—so I've ripped out the TVs, don't allow the internet in my house, and don't let my kids have cell phones." Sadly, these parents have mistaken technology and hardware as the problem. The problem isn't the technology—it's the way we use it, and the way we allow others to misuse it in our homes. Instead of banning everything, we should harness the good, and filter out the bad. We should set limits but not shut down access.

You can and should relax, but without letting down your guard. You must also have hard and fast rules, without turning your house into a boot camp. How you describe and teach your standards is just as important in protecting your children as the rules and safeguards you adopt for your family. Take this advice from Shannon, who shares how to say "yes" and "no" to younger children:

"I try to say 'yes' as often as possible—even when it's 'Yes, we can do that tomorrow' (rather than right this minute). Or, 'Yes, you may have 5 raisins,' (rather than the 300 they want). Or, 'Yes, you can watch a movie after we pick up the toys together.' And when I have to say, 'No,' I try to keep my voice cheerful and my face loving—after all, the refusal is about the stuff rather than about the child. 'No, you can't have another popsicle now. Nope. Nope. Nope.' And my little ones will usually smile back. And when they continue to ask, I try to stay cheerful and say 'Nope! But we can read a story, and if you are hungry you can have ____ or ____.' And if they are still asking, I'll say, 'What's the answer to that question?' I try to save the mean face for when there is defiance of me or meanness to each other or dangerous behavior.

Make Your Home Inviting, Warm, and . . . Fun!

And when I give directions and parameters, I phrase them positively as often as possible, as in, 'Clean up the spill.' (Telling them not to spill is just a ludicrous idea.) 'Talk, please.' (Instead of 'don't whine!')

Shannon's advice can be broadened to teenagers, too. "Yes, you can have friends over—but you have to do your homework first." "Yes, you can go to the movies after you help me clean up."

It's all about *your* attitude. Sometimes we let our teenager's attitude control the mood of our home. What a mistake! With their developing emotions, raging hormones, and fluctuating biological moods, it's important that Mom and Dad be the steady, calm force of reason. You've probably heard the saying, "If Mamma ain't happy, ain't anybody happy." Truer words were never spoken! The mom sets the tone for the home. You can be the mean principal or the sweet, inspirational teacher. You can be the one your kids fear, or the one they come to for advice. Of course, this applies to fathers, too. The bottom line is that if we allow our kids to set the tone of the home, it will be an emotional cyclone. And if we operate with frustration or weariness, our entire home and everyone in it will become miserable in minutes, regardless of how care-free they were when they walked in the door. But if we set a tone of joy and hope, the home will be a more inviting place for everyone.

Jim shared an important point on demeanor in his e-mail: *"I am reminded of something John Cleese said. 'People often confuse being serious with being somber.' I'm always a serious dad. I'm also seriously very happy with my girls. I am often seriously playful out at the park or in the pool. I can be and often am somber too, as the situation warrants. But that's up to the situation, not a 'Sarge' state of mind."*

Make your home. . . . fun! When my kids were little, my husband and I made a decision to create an atmosphere where they and their friends would want to play. We called our house, "The Popsicle House"—meaning that in the steamy days of summer, the little kids in the neighborhood knew there was always a cold, delicious Popsicle or two awaiting them at the Hagelins. We took great delight in watching their little eyes light up and their faces beam as they took the melting, colorful pop from our hands. It was a glorious pleasure to hear them smack their lips and giggle with delight with every slurp. And of course, there was the clean-up: I must have helped wash a thousand little sticky hands and wiped down just as many stained and smiling cheeks.

Our door was always open to the neighborhood children, and it must have slammed shut a million times a day. We often had dirty fingerprints and footprints adorning the walls and floors. But there was also a lot of laughter, running, and creativity blooming within our walls. How I cherish those memories!

We've also always stocked our home and yard with plenty of gadgets, art supplies, and costumes. We've kept a stock of bikes over the years (many purchased at yard sales), skateboards, and just about every other kind of kid-powered transportation you can imagine (when they were little we had Big Wheels, little red wagons, and trikes). Although we've never been blessed with a swimming pool, that hasn't kept our kids and us from getting wet. Summertime saw our yard marked with snaking hoses and sprinklers and the blur of water balloons flying in mid-air or splashing on some squealing child's back. Summer nights often found our kids and their friends gathered around campfires in the backyard—complete with marshmallows, hot dogs, and soda. The sounds of crickets and the gentle breezes were often punctuated by the war cries and hysterical laughter associated with shaving cream fights or mischievous games of "Ring and Run" (ringing the doorbell of a friendly neighbor and running away or hiding around the corner. Little did my kids know I usually called my friends first to warn them that the fun was about to begin). We've had tree-houses, wooden bridges hanging between huge trees, playhouses, and forts in which epic battles took place.

As our children grew into teens, we were always very careful to change the environment with their ever-developing and changing interests. The basements and garages of our various homes have been transformed from "garage band" practice rooms, to silk-screening and art studios, and to photography dark rooms. We have purchased foosball tables from Craigslist (a website for locals to connect and sell items), art equipment from e-bay, and countless video games, guitars, and other "fun stuff" from pawn shops. We've "invested" in a movie library, VCR and DVD players, and classic board games.

And the kids keep on coming. My happiest moments come when my home is filled with the banter of teenagers—whether it's in the middle of the night during a sleepover of chatty girls, or on a Saturday afternoon when the guys have gathered for another delightfully noisy band practice. I am truly blessed to have had the opportunity to get to know my children's friends, and to know that they enjoy hanging out at our home.

Feed them, and they will come. I've already mentioned the Popsicles and campfire foods, but honestly, I can't make this point enough times: kids and teenagers love food. It is an important part of their social gatherings, and if your home isn't known for having it, you will have a lonely life, indeed. On the other hand, if your home is filled with what kids crave, they will come.

Years ago, my husband and I dedicated a substantial part of our budget for the feeding of the masses—specifically, the masses of kids we hoped would fill our home. We save pizza coupons, cram our freezers and pantry with "two-for-one" sales on ice cream, sodas, and chips, and always have jars of colorful candy in more than one room at a time. OK—so at this point you're probably wondering about the eating habits we encourage. I've got to admit, since we feed our children healthy meals the vast majority of the time, I've never been one of those to worry too much about weekend grazing! We bake cookies, brownies, and cakes. We have make-your-own ice cream sundae bars, and have purchased every kind of chip you can imagine. I am a "supplier" of junk food, and I'm proud of it!

Weight has never been a problem for our children because we also make sure they get plenty of exercise in organized sports, bicycling, and running around the neighborhood. They aren't allowed to just sit around and watch hours upon hours of television. There are just too many fun experiences awaiting the child whose imagination is not stifled by canned television programming. Food isn't the enemy—it's the consumption of too much of the wrong kind accompanied by laziness or inactivity that robs our kids of their best health.

Create opportunities to interact. Of course, when your home is filled with children or teenagers, adult supervision is imperative. But just "being there" isn't enough. It's far more effective and enjoyable for everyone if you become a natural part of the activity than it is to be the "secret police" slipping around every corner. Be bold about your presence—but not intrusive. Let visitors know what rooms are off limits, and of course, what behavior is and isn't acceptable. And most importantly, look for opportunities to interact and get to know the kids in your home. Engage them in conversation, and let them know that you are truly interested in them and their lives. You just never know when you might make a life-long friend, help shape a destiny, or even learn something from the younger generation.

Make Your Home Inviting, Warm, and...Fun!

Date _____

   Today I decided to adopt a tone—and a style—for my home that would make it a warm, inviting place for my children and their friends.

_____

Signature

Some ideas for making my home more inviting are:

_____

_____

_____

_____

_____

_____

MORE HELP

HAPPY HOUSEWIVES CLUB (happyhousewivesclub.com)

Darla Shine created the Happy Housewives Club after deciding to trade her briefcase for a diaper bag and discovering a lack of respect for the hard work of stay at home parenting. It is an invaluable resource for every parent. She covers topics from fitness and working from home, to crafts for kids and healthy meals. I highly recommend checking out her creative site.

Create Family Time

THE CHALLENGE

Do you know your family?

You may think that's a silly question. "Of course we know each other," many parents would reply. "We live under the same roof. We see each other daily. We go on vacations together. How could we not know each other?"

Some research, however, suggests that many parents and their children are, in an important sense, almost strangers.

One major study, sponsored by the Alfred P. Sloan Foundation, comes from the UCLA Center on Everyday Lives of Families—and it paints a portrait of family life in crisis. It reports that the time many families spend together is crammed with wall-to-wall activities.

Mothers and fathers ferry their kids feverishly about—a play date here, a practice there, not a moment to spare—tethered by cell phones and sustained by meals on the run. You can't really know your children if all of your time with them is spent running to and fro in a frenetic whirlwind. Genuine intimacy is impossible under such conditions.

Of course, there's nothing wrong with activities *per se.* Nobody's saying kids should just sit at home. Involvement in sports, for example, is incredibly beneficial for children—especially teens. Take it from a mother who's cheered her sons at track meets and baseball games. I counted it a blessing that my son spent many of his high-school Friday nights at five-hour track meets, with no time *or* energy left for mischief. And, it was far better to have him exhausted from track practice after school than sitting around thinking about girls all afternoon!

But it's critical to stop and reflect on what might be missing in their lives—the most important physical "thing" to their development: you.

This isn't mere sentiment talking. It's a matter of social science. NewsMax.com reported a study conducted by The Associated Press and (believe it or not) MTV, found that spending time with family was the number one activity that kids between 13 and 24 said makes them happy. It makes a huge difference.

Take something as simple as the family dinner. Sure, it's nice, but who on Earth has time? The bottom line is, if you want to help your children avoid a host of problems, you will *make* time.

In our household, especially when three teenagers were living at home, we designated nights when we would eat together and told our kids, "Your friends are welcome to join us." This firm but inclusive directive made for many now-treasured evenings when we bonded with our children and their friends. I know in my mother's heart that the time, laughs, and discussions had a powerful impact on all of them. And the data supports my hunch: One study from the National Center of Addiction and Substance Abuse at Columbia University found a connection between "frequent family dinners" and lower rates of teen smoking, drinking, and drug use. Specifically:

> Compared with teens who frequently had dinner with their families, (five nights or more per week) those who had dinner with their families only two nights per week or less were twice as likely to be involved in substance abuse. They were 2.5 times as likely to smoke cigarettes, more than 1.5 times as likely to drink alcohol, and nearly three times as likely to try marijuana.

Just your "being there" also helps your children. A comprehensive study, drawing on data from the National Longitudinal Study of Adolescent Health and published in the *Journal of the American Medical Association*, notes that "teenagers were less likely to experience emotional distress if their parents were in the home when they awoke, when they came home from school, at dinnertime, and when they went to bed, if they engaged in activities with their parents, and if their parents had high expectations regarding their academic performance."

It makes sense when you think about it. After all, if you are available for and nearby your children, even if you don't "do" anything in the conventional sense of the word, your presence sends the undeniable message: "I care about you enough to be here."

And what about single parents? The bottom line is, your job is harder. But it is not impossible. You must find allies in the battle—other adults who share your values and will support you and help you raise your child to be all he was meant to be. I've dedicated an entire chapter on the importance of joining hearts and hands with other adults in this adventure we call "parenthood"—it's called "Secure Allies in the Battle"—please read it. Being a single parent doesn't mean you do it alone. Don't give up, give in, or become discouraged. You can raise wonderful, happy children.

Another study, published in the journal *Family Relations*, certainly caught my maternal eye. It noted that children who succeed in school tend to have mothers "who frequently talk and listen to them." Fathers, too, make quite a difference. Here's how familyfacts.org sums up a study on the impact of dads reported in the *Journal of Marriage and the Family*: "Compared to peers with less paternal attention, children whose fathers spent leisure time, shared meals, helped with homework or reading, and engaged in other home activities with them have significantly higher levels of academic performance."

The pop culture frequently portrays dads as disposable, doltish, or dangerous. The reality, of course, is that dads play a vital role in their children's development and well-being. One study reveals that "father absence was associated with the likelihood that adolescent girls will be sexually active and become pregnant as teenagers." Many other studies reveal the essential person that "dad" is in the lives of his children.

And what about Mom? It has been said that the most powerful word in any language is "mother." Yet our society increasingly belittles the role and seems to place higher value on the mom who hires others to care for her children than the mom who sacrifices to raise them herself. One study, published in *Family Relations*, found that the children who were the most successful in first grade (in terms of test scores and teachers' ratings) were those whose mothers had spent "a great deal of time in positive interactions with them." It also found that their academic success "correlated with their mothers' involvement in talking with them, listening to them and answering their questions."

We know the importance of maintaining a balanced diet for good physical health. The UCLA study shows that it's just as crucial, for the sake of our mental and emotional health, to lead a balanced life.

And how do we restore balance to our frantic family lives? Make a point of injecting some downtime into it—heck, schedule it. Go for a walk—not a power walk, but a slow one. Play a game together, preferably a board or card game, with everyone sitting around the table and interacting.

Realize, too, that not every activity must involve the whole group. Take that walk or play that game with one son or one daughter. Give everybody a turn. In time, you'll find yourself having real conversations with the people who matter most. And don't neglect your spouse! A regular date can really help strengthen your marriage.

It's hard, too, to overemphasize the importance of having dinner together—sitting down, away from the television, as a group—as often as possible. The potential it affords to impart lessons in courtesy, hash out problems, or just have a good laugh is unmatched.

Reviving this balance is also crucial to one's spiritual health. It's all too easy, when every minute of our day is jam-packed, to neglect church and daily prayer. Big mistake. Only by slowing down can we hope to really hear the voice of God. Taking a formal retreat occasionally is a fine idea, but we also need the "mini-retreats" that God uses to recharge our batteries when we take time to talk with and visit Him.

If you're feeling overscheduled, look at your family's time and how it's spent. Get together and discuss ways to pare back on outside activities and make more time for each other. One fair way to take more control of family time is to set the number of activities each child can do in a school year. Instead of track, drama, tennis, football, soccer, and horseback riding for each child—leaving you the frazzled chauffer struggling to fit everything in—let each child choose two or three activities for the year when school starts. And stick to it when the new seasons begin. In addition to lightening up your schedule, this method will also help teach your children about priorities and time management.

It's crucial that we make time for what is truly important—not merely so we can fashion some pleasant memories, but so we can raise our kids to soar above the toxic culture and to become the men and women God intends for them to be.

Mom and Dad, you are vital. The culture won't tell you that, but the facts, your gut, and your kids' lives testify to your power. Your opportunity to enjoy them when they're small and to shape them when they become teens will disappear before your eyes. Take it from a mom who knows.

Don't just give your family *things*. Give yourself. You'll get far more back than you can possibly imagine.

IN YOUR SHOES

You can even try things that seem drastic:

Several years ago one cold winter month my family's frantically busy life came to a screeching halt: we became quitters. Ok, so not really quitters—but we did cancel every scheduled event for two weeks. What a beautiful two weeks that turned out to be! Instead of rushing from piano to ballet to Scouts to...whatever, we abruptly stopped in the middle of the mayhem and did something radical—spent evenings together. After school work was done, we gathered around the fireplace and drank hot chocolate and just talked to each other. Some evenings found us lounging on the couch and floor, with each person quietly reading a book, magazine, or simply sketching. There was no clock-watching, no exhaustion, and no tension—we were the Masters of our Universe. After our brief family sabbatical we were more deliberate about the activities we picked-up again, and our entrance back into the social scene found us well-rested and more reflective. Those two weeks changed my life as a mother, and I emerged with a greater sense of purpose in using both my and my children's time more wisely

When my son Nick left for college in the fall of 2007. I wrote about it as a sobering moment that left me very thankful for all the time we spent together:

My husband and I held each other and cried more than I think we had in years of marriage. We left our son, Nick, alone in his dorm room, far from home, after nurturing and loving him for eighteen years. Our little boy is now a tall, responsible young man facing life on his own. Yes, it's what good parents everywhere dream of and want for their kids—to become independent adults who fly from our arms into a world where they can make their own mark. But still, the tears come—for me, mainly because I now know from painful personal experience that there is a certain brevity to childhood. Those wild and wonderful days have vanished forever.

I thank God for the five years we home-schooled, for the opportunity I had to work from a home office, and for the fact that my husband has always put family ahead of work. I'm grateful for the nights I said prayers with Nick and tucked him into bed, for the hours spent helping with homework, listening to teenage rants, attending endless track meets, and for watching him learn from his mistakes. Basically, I'm thankful for every second I spent with my boy. It's still difficult to see him go.

It doesn't help a bit that we went through this just one year ago when we left our first son, Drew, at college. In fact, this time is worse—there are now two empty beds and two sons whose laughter I won't hear around the house anymore. Nick and Drew's childish antics and boyhood ways are gone. What remains are the memories and one precious 15-year-old daughter who is probably a bit nervous about all the attention she will be getting. (It's kind of funny, in a sad sort of way.) I've promised myself that I will continue to give her the gradually increasing amount of freedom teens need—but I've also vowed anew that I won't let modern society dictate what that means.

• • •

As I was writing this chapter I had to come to a very hard realization about my own life: I had allowed great causes and great opportunities to creep into my family life and crowd out time I should have been spending with my own teens. As the years went on and the causes I believed in grew more urgent, it was too easy to go to "one more meeting" in the late afternoon, or attend just "one more event" in the evening. My blackberry was my constant companion and many times when I was with my family, my mind was actually somewhere else.

There it was: I, the one who gave up career advances, home schooled, and deliberately moved away from the big city to raise my children in a real neighborhood with a slower pace when they were small, had somehow managed get overcommitted outside the home when they became teenagers. Writing this book caused me to stop and evaluate my own life, and I'm so glad I did. I decided to step aside as a vice president of The Heritage Foundation and take on a new role that would allow me to work from home with the vast majority of the tasks complete by the time my daughter walks in the door from school. In the world's eyes, it was probably a foolish decision—one doesn't just walk away from being a vice president of The Heritage Foundation—especially in the uncertain economic times in which we live. But my husband and I de-cided that it was what we must do. And so we did. When I told our sixteen-year-old daughter the plan, she jumped off the bed and threw her arms around my neck. Wow. What confirmation! Good causes and careers will always be waiting for us after our children have gone. But childhood and the teenage years wait for no one.

I'm not saying every mom or dad should change or quit their jobs! I am saying that you should constantly evaluate and re-evaluate how you are spending your time when you are not with your family. Is it worth it! Have you become a victim of "mission creep," either by your career or your volunteer activities! Can you afford to slow down—can your kids afford for you not to! Is this the time your children need you more than you need the extra income! These are not questions society teaches us to ask—but if we don't, when our children grow up and leave our homes, we could be left with a lifetime of regret for not having asked those difficult questions.

ACT NOW

Date _____

Today I started looking for ways to increase the amount of time I spend with my children. I pledge to make that time as meaningful and enjoyable as I can—and to show my children, by my very presence, that they mean more to me than anyone else in the world.

_____
Signature

MORE HELP

FAMILYFACTS.ORG: Looking for scientific data about families? You'll find a solid resource in this free web site from The Heritage Foundation. Familyfacts.org is a clearinghouse of useful, reliable information distilled from numerous studies and academic journals worldwide. The findings from lengthy reports are boiled down into bite-sized blocks that are easy to understand.

You can find many Web sites suggesting ways to expand and improve your time together, but here are three to get you started:

FAMILYTIME.COM: Family Time is filled with cooking ideas, fun family activities, helpful reminders, money-saving offers, and more. You can try the "recipe of the day," follow their tips for decorating or organizing your home, or get some pointers for creating a family garden.

FAMILIESWITHPURPOSE.COM: You'll find loads of tips at the "Families With Purpose" web site. "Family activities don't have to be elaborate, expensive planned out ideas," the group notes. "Sometimes, simple is better. Kids are looking for your time and attention, so don't forget the simple things in life:

- Read a book together
- Fly a kite
- Bake cookies
- Go fishing
- Plant flowers
- Build a tent and eat lunch inside
- Go for a walk
- Shoot hoops or play catch
- Play hide and seek
- Catch fireflies

continued

Create Family Time

MAKEMEALTIMEFAMILYTIME.COM: As you might guess, this web site talks about the benefits of eating together. It even allows you to download a free set of "mealtime conversation cards."

FAMILYLIFE.COM—This site, run by Family Life Today, contains tons of free resources on how to improve both the quality and quantity of your family life together. You can also sign-up to receive e-mails filled with helpful tips on family living.

FAMILY.ORG—The go-to experts for all things related to faith and family, this site by Focus on the Family is your one-stop shop for videos, tools, books, free research, and counseling. It is a must-visit-often site if you are serious about making your family the strongest it can be.

Discuss The Modern Challenges Of Friendship With Your Teen And Evaluate Your Own Friendships

THE CHALLENGE

This isn't rocket science: teenagers are social creatures and want to be respected by their peers, surrounded by "friends," and invited to all the right parties. The need for acceptance is tremendously high in the pre-teen and teenage years, and peer pressure is omnipresent. But in today's world, finding loyal friends who share high values is more difficult and risky than creating rockets—it's more like heart surgery.

The pressures and subject matter that your child might have to deal with are far greater than what you and I had to face, or any generation before us. Here are just three of the difficult issues involving friendship that are unique to our generation of children:

Absentee Parents: With so many households run by over-stressed single parents or homes with two parents who work long hours, there is often a serious lack of adult supervision and interaction. These days, instead of parents teaching values, it's often the sexualized media that is teaching our kids' friends what is and isn't acceptable. The resulting onslaught of sexual promiscuity, teen pregnancy, and the proliferation of porn, means the chances are very high that the kids your sons and daughters are hanging out with may have serious personal problems. Others may come from homes that haven't yet had their eyes opened to the dangers of the culture.

Brokenness: The breakdown of the family in the last thirty years is stunning. For every one hundred children born in the United States, sixty are born to a broken home. That means they are either born to a single parent or to a family that will suffer from divorce. So many children come from fractured families that it might be difficult for your child to find friends who haven't been deeply wounded by the tragedy of divorce. Many teens today have no one at home modeling what basic family commitment, fidelity, and marriage are—let alone friendship. In broken homes, often no one circles back around to the children to provide counseling and therapy. Our society still hasn't quite figured out how to help children through this pain. Social Science researcher Pat Fagan says that ours has become a "culture of rejection." What a sad environment in which to grow up. The result is an entire generation of young people who are searching for help and meaning through their loneliness and heartache. And since even the most wonderful families and adults in the world are incredibly busy, it might just be that your child finds himself counseling a friend through great heartaches. But our kids were not intended—nor are they qualified—to bear such burdens.

"Me, Me, Me": Society is fighting against us as parents and pushing our children into a "me first" saturated world. The "me, me, me" mentality teaches our kids that people are rarely good for anything more than what they can give us. Our children are told to look-out for themselves and get what they can, even if it is at the expense of others. They are fed an almost constant message that tells them to obtain whatever makes them happy—whether it's money, cool clothes, popularity, or dating—the list goes on and on. And they're shown that treating anyone who gets in their way with contempt or rudeness is not only okay, it's often portrayed as funny.

There are two critical steps parents must take in helping our pre-teens and teens navigate these uncharted waters of friendship. The first is to spend a lot of time talking with your kids about the challenges they face with their peers. The second is to model friendship ourselves. The easiest way for your children to understand the meaning of true friendship is to see it modeled first-hand in you. With the typical challenges that teens face in forming friendships compounded by the issues mentioned above, it's more important than ever for parents to take an active role in helping teach our children about friendship and in watching how we provide for and select friendships in our own lives. If we don't model friendship in front of them, then how will they ever learn what true friendship looks like? From TV and the movies they watch?

FROM MY HOME TO YOURS

The following tips are designed to help you discuss and handle the unique situations described above.

- Should your son or daughter suddenly abandon a friend who begins to suffer from depression over his "dead beat dad" or "missing mom"? No—but your child needs to know that he is not expected to handle the situation by himself. Make sure you know the family situations that your children's friends come from (See Chapter 14, "Secure Allies in the Battle"). For those kids who come from single-parent homes, make sure you've spent time talking to the parent to see what the needs are. Don't ever put your child in a situation where they have to be the counselor. Make sure your son or daughter knows that they are to always respond in love, but that if they sense depression, extreme loneliness, or heartache in their friend, they are to let you know right away. You should then circle back to the parent and provide support or even recommend professional counseling.

■ There's a verse in the Bible that says, "He who walks with the wise grows wise but a companion of fools suffers harm." Another one states, "Bad company corrupts good character." Even those with no faith can testify to the truth of these statements. You must be very deliberate in teaching your kids how to choose friends wisely and how to surround themselves with good company instead of bad. Teach them the character qualities they should be seeking in their friends—loyalty, kindness, respect toward their parents and others in authority, and honesty, to name a few. Be actively involved in knowing who they hang out with at school, at the mall, and at church. Get to know the parents of their friends and build relationships with those families. It's up to us to protect our kids from "fools" and teach them how to walk among those who are wise.

■ And what do you do when your teen's friend has become involved in sexual activity, drinking, or other harmful behavior? First, step in right away and protect your child.

Second, connect with an adult in that child's life. I know of one mother who found out recently that her daughter's best friend was sneaking out at night to sleep with her boyfriend. This woman was obviously troubled by the situation, but didn't know what she should do. I simply said, "If it was Kathy slipping out at night, wouldn't you want someone to tell you?" She got my point and then faced the difficult action of having to call the girl's mother to discuss the rumor. The mother was devastated, but not as much as she would have been if the daughter had gotten pregnant or hurt in her late-night jaunts.

It's critical in these circumstances to let your son or daughter know that there are times when friendships must be cut off. Your first priority is your child's well-being, and we all know that even the best of kids can be pulled down by their friends. Author Lindy Keffer recently wrote an article about friendship for *Beyond Brio* magazine, a wonderful monthly publication for older teenage girls. In, "We're All Broken" she talks directly to teenagers and offers great advice—you may want to use it as a guide when talking to your son or daughter about the difference between being kind, and opening your heart to be a friend:

"If you're hanging out with someone who makes excuses for her failures or who promises to change but never acts on it, chances are you've got bad company. Either way, you're still called to love that person. But loving someone who's a bad influence doesn't mean sharing the intimate parts of your life with her. It means being kind when you pass in the halls. It means not gossiping. Those are loving things you can do without getting pulled down by a bad influence."

■ Set the example of what true friendships look like. Mom and Dad, this might be a little tough for you, but maybe it's time to evaluate who you spend time with. Are they the type of people you want your own children to look at as what a friend should be? Do they provide strength, encouragement, comfort, and peace? Or are they more prone to complain, drain you, and criticize others? Maybe it's time to spend less time with those whose values you don't really share, and seek out those whose values you do.

And be extra-sensitive about how you behave with your friends. Given the number of marital problems today, a popular activity among women is to meet at Starbucks and complain about their husbands. Refuse to do this. Absolutely refuse—whether your children are with you or not. You should spend time with women who help strengthen your marriage, not feed anxiety or trouble.

Another key point for moms to examine is how we talk about our friends when they aren't around. If you are constantly "dissing" your friends in front of your children, your kids will wonder just what kind of person you really are. The silent thoughts that will go through their minds are, "If she's so bad, why is mom hanging out with her?" and, "I didn't know my mom could be so critical of people she says are her friends."

■ Dads—a special word to you: Be a strong enough father that you are willing to maintain only those friendships that make you a better person. Your role as a good husband and father is critical in today's world. If you have friends who compromise your integrity in your children's eyes, you will be less effective in forming those hearts entrusted to your care. Teen guys and girls especially need to see men of character in action. So don't spend "guys night out" whooping it up with your friends. Don't use foul language with your buddies when you're shooting the breeze. And do find other men who can help build your faith.

You might want to consider joining an organization like "Promise Keepers" (promisekeepers.org) that is designed to help men be loyal, true, and the primary influencers on their families. Make sure that the guys you hang out with are men that you would be proud for your sons and daughters to know as you know them.

IN YOUR SHOES

I have a teenage daughter who has many great friends who have hung out en masse at our home over the years. But you know how catty pre-teen and teenage girls can be. As they started entering their teen years I established a hard and fast rule in our home: you are not permitted to trash and criticize girls who aren't around. Period. No "talking about" your friends behind their backs. I always explained to Kristin that if she refused to engage in such banter, then all of her friends would soon figure out that she would never talk badly about them when they weren't around either.

• • •

A few years ago, my best childhood friend Suzanne Ebel and I decided to celebrate our 40th birthdays together. We took a long weekend trip to Chicago and included our pre-teen daughters in the festivities. The four of us spent 72 hours doing "girlie" stuff like shopping and lunching and laughing. All three nights found us up into the wee hours talking about warm memories of our moms, our friendship as children, and

*giggling like crazy over distant teen crushes on boys. We spoke
freely of our faith as young women and how we made it a
point to encourage each other. We spoke about how much we
valued and counted on our loyalty to each other, and how important that bond was when we often faced those who made
fun of our strong Christian values. Our girls sat in rapt attention in their pajamas and listened to every word. The weekend
was a blast and a great way to celebrate our birthdays, but
more importantly, Suzanne and I were able to show our girls
the priceless treasure of a true and lasting friendship.*

ACT NOW

Date _____

Today I began talking to my kids about the unique challenges they face
in the world of friendship, and I started evaluating how I model friendship
for them.

_____
Signature

Know The Difference Between Your *Principles* And Your *Preferences*

THE CHALLENGE

In our world, right is often declared "wrong," and wrong is declared "right"; materialism and position are valued more highly than character and commitment; and styles, music, and what is "socially acceptable" change faster than the speed of sound. It's no wonder that our preferences often take front-and-center in our lives, causing us to be blind to the fact that adhering to a solid code of principles is the compass that will guide us through the ever-shifting winds of "trends."

Know the difference between what you believe in, and what you prefer in a given moment.

Principles are the foundation upon which you stand. They are the standards by which you live. They are the things worth sacrificing and fighting, and sometimes, even dying for. Principles are the beliefs on which you will not compromise—no matter what. Principles are the foundation for achieving the vision you have for your children. (Remember that vision you wrote down?)

Preferences, on the other hand, are things you can (and should) give up if the cost of having them is greater than the cost of setting them aside. They are the items you forsake for the sake of another. They are the styles and trends mentioned above that often confuse us about what is truly important. Preferences are the first "me" in "me, me, me." There is nothing wrong with having preferences or in getting them. But when securing what we want becomes more important than practicing what we believe, then we've got a new "p" to worry about—problems.

When I was a teenager, a woman named Joyce Strader often reminded me to "never sacrifice the permanent on the altar of the temporary." I've thought about her wise admonishment many times during my life, and am so grateful she cared enough to remind us that the choices and compromises we make today based on selfishness or mere desire can damage things that are lasting like our conscience, our character, and even our reputation.

FROM MY HOME TO YOURS

Take the time to write down a list of principles that should guide your life, and then compare each one to a preference that might relate to it. For example:

My preference is that my daughter will make all A's in high school.
But....
My principle is that she will always do her best.

My preference is that my son will have a haircut that my friends like.

But....
My principle is that he will be clean.

My preference is that my daughter will be popular among her peers.
But ...
My principle is that she will always stand for virtue, honesty, and truth.

My preference is that we will be efficient and tactical in the way we run our home.
But...
My principle is to create an environment that fosters the belief that mistakes can be redeemed.

My preference is to "just get along" with everyone.
But...
My principle is to stand up for what I believe in.

My preference is to be a cool mom.
But....
My principle is to challenge my children to tower above the toxic culture.

Sit down with each of your children and help them make a list, too. Then go over what might be missing. At the end of the exercise, you'll have a pretty good road-map filled with warning signals about what circumstances might be difficult for you or them. Discuss what those situations might be, and then develop a plan for your child on how to avoid them. You should also be aware that your son or daughter might find themselves in situations they haven't planned on, that just might cause them to forgo a principle due to temptation. You should discuss the likelihood of falling into one of these temptation traps, and then talk about how your child can avoid getting into them in the first place. For instance, if you have a teenage son, one of his preferences when he is on a date with a hot girl could end up being that he prefers to "make out" with her—even though his principle is to remain sexually pure and be respectful of women. When faced with such a choice in the heat of passion, what do you think the likelihood of his choosing to uphold his principle is? Um . . . probably not so good. But if you've taken the initiative to discuss it with him in advance, when there is no "hot temptation" cuddled up next to him in a dark car, then you can help him avoid making a huge mistake. Teach him to avoid placing himself in the situation at all—he should decide well in advance to be involved in group dates and to avoid being alone with his heart-throb in a secluded area. This is where curfews are helpful, too. In other words, help him understand that boundaries and decisions made early in the evening can help him uphold his core principles later on.

Train your child and yourself to think about principles when you find yourself in a quandary or when you feel confused about what you should do. The idea is to remember to think first about the principle that is involved. Then ask yourself, "If I get my preference (or my desire), will it do harm to the life-principle I want to uphold?"

IN YOUR SHOES

I received this powerful story from a father on how he will never regret standing for one of his principles in the midst of a dire situation:

One of the biggest principles I have tried to practice with my son, Ken, is that I will always trust him unless he has shown that he cannot be trusted. When he was 16 years old, he was involved in what I thought was a minor lapse of judgment during school hours with several other boys. During lunch, when they have off-campus privileges, the boys went into a dilapidated vacant house . . . despite the obvious "no trespassing" signs plastered all over the walls. A curious neighbor called the county and soon the house was swarming with police. Fortunately, Ken's inner voice had told him about fifteen minutes earlier that he should leave the house. So when the officers started arresting the young men, my boy was long gone. However, with reports that he had been there, and that one kid had been seen running away after the police arrived, Ken fell under immediate suspicion for two serious offenses—resisting arrest and fleeing the scene of a crime. The circumstantial evidence looked pretty bad. But Ken told me, the school principal, and the investigating officer that he had walked in the house, stayed for a few minutes, and then left because he knew he shouldn't be there. He insisted that he was not there when the police arrived so he could not have possibly been the one running away. I had my doubts, but again, my principle had been to build honesty and integrity into my son by showing that I would always default to a position of faith in him—unless or until he proved otherwise. It was tough to adhere to that principle, given the circumstances. Outwardly I was supporting my son and his character with the police—but inwardly I was dying a thousand deaths from near despair that it was possible that he might now be compounding a horrible situation by lying about it to school and law enforcement officials. Fortunately for Ken, and me, more information soon came to light, and the guilty student was identified and confessed. The lesson this taught me was that my principle of placing trust in my son in a visible manner was worth the risk. Ken learned to obey signs, but much more than that, he learned that I had not lied when I said that I would always stand by him, ready to protect his good name and his integrity.

I know from experience how failing to uphold your principles can cause regret:

The trip was meant to be a bonding time for my daughter and me. Our favorite place in the world is a small, bridgeless paradise along the Gulf Coast of Florida known as Little Gasparilla Island. Kristin and I went there for a week one summer—just the two of us. We love the warm, turquoise waters, the white sandy beaches, and the abundance of marine life. A key goal of the trip was to rent a jet ski for the day to explore the waters of the Intracoastal Waterway and the canals and passes that lead to the ocean—and in so doing, to have a great adventure by just being together.

As soon as we got hold of that Jet Ski we started flying at what seemed to be light speed over the waves of the Gulf, bouncing and clinging for dear life. Kristin and I took turns at the wheel—which means I endured hours of fear that I just might go reeling off the back of that thing and crash into the churning waters with maximum impact while Kristin continued barreling away at breakneck speed. I learned very quickly that she is much more daring and confident than I. She knows how to cut the jet ski sharply in any direction and take a wave head on, propelling us into the air and slamming us back down as we lurch ever forward. It is a great ride whenever Kristin is driving—but I wonder why she isn't deaf, as I am prone to fits of uncontrollable high-pitched screams and squeals when she is in command!

Later in the day we beached the water bike on the end of the island and hopped off to look for shells and just sit awhile. It was glorious. When we got hungry we decided to jet down the canal to a paradise called Palm Island. Tucked away in the middle of a snaking lagoon and behind clumps of man-

groves, the dock that serves as the landing spot for the delightful restaurant awaited us. The problem is, when you dock a watercraft, you have to tie it up carefully so it doesn't float away. Or, worse yet, tie it up too loosely at low tide only to find that your boat or jet ski was pushed by the current under the dock with the rising tide and then crushed as the water continued to steadily lift it. To be sure, it was during this process of tying down the 20,000 dollar Jet Ski (that belonged to someone else) that I came pretty close to wrecking the entire day. Although I've been an island girl my entire life, I've never quite been able to get this docking and tying event down. And even though my husband is an excellent sailor, Kristin is a novice at the knotting thing, too. As we were tying off the boat, I had determined there was a very specific piling Kristin's end should be anchored on. Not wanting to give her a direct command to tie it there, I said several times that it "might be a good idea to try it over there." This was really my way of telling her what I thought she should do without actually telling her what to do—if you know what I mean. But Kristin was still figuring out where she thought it would be safest to anchor it, her beautiful head calculating the many factors that would lead to success or disaster. While we worked to steady the craft and brace it from the motion of the ever-lapping waters that insisted on banging it into the side of the dock, the stress began to build. We also had the added treat of working with ropes that were way too long—by about five feet. So there we were—one teenager with developing emotions and growing independence, and one forty-something slightly stressed mom who was also a bit hot and hungry— trying to figure out how to get this craft that didn't belong to us from getting crushed. (Which would have also, by the way, left us stranded on the island and at the mercy of the owner who would have had to close his shop several miles away in order to come rescue us by boat. But, no pressure.) Anyway, after some time I totally and completely blew it. I said, "Kristin, I've told you three times to tie the rope around that post and you just keep disobeying." Well, I might as well have told her that her best friend had just betrayed her.

What had been a problem-solving, team-building, bonding moment was obliterated. Kristin silently began tying up the Jet Ski where I said she should as tear-filled eyes and sadness enveloped her lovely face.

Because I preferred to satisfy my immediate desire for food and comfort over practicing my principle to be patient with my kids, I cast a cloud over the otherwise sunny day and darkened my daughter's tender spirit.

Thankfully, we both believe in repentance, forgiveness, and redemption, so when I finally humbled myself and said I was so sorry, she heaped love and compassion on me. The day ended with us reunited, sitting on the beach absorbing the incredible beauty of another dazzling sunset. But I lost a few precious hours that day with my daughter that are now gone forever.

ACT NOW

Date _____

Today I began listing the principles I want to live out and instill in my children, and have pledged to do my best to never sacrifice them for the sake of convenience, desire, or doubt.

_____
Signature

Write A Letter
To Your Teen

THE CHALLENGE

As children turn into teens, many parents find it difficult to express the deep love, warmth, and vision that we have for them. The fact is, a sullen teenager is hard to connect with! As moms and dads, we often forget that what our teens crave more than anything is genuine love, thoughtful words, and encouragement from us. Their peers aren't prone to provide the affirmation they need—and the culture seems to do everything possible to supply plenty of just the opposite. But when we relinquish our power to encourage and advise them, we only contribute to their tendency of withdrawal and angst. The hopeful news is that research shows that teens desperately want parental affirmation, approval, and love. Although they may appear to be like bricks—

cold and indifferent to your advice and counsel—they are actually more like seeds that are capable of tremendous growth when planted in a nurturing environment and constantly watered with words of love, encouragement, and counsel. Such words are never more powerful than when they are written down. But, my goodness, how many parents have ever written their child a single letter? My guess is that most moms and dads have never penned more than a few words on a birthday card. As valuable as those cards may be, they are not enough.

Obviously, it's critical to begin building more time and discussion with your child into your day (see Chapter 12, "Learn How to Have Meaningful Discussions with Your Child"). But in the meantime, there is something you can do to start bridging the communication gap and showing your teens just how much they mean to you: Write them a love letter.

It's one thing to talk to your kids—but writing down your feelings and sharing the vision you have for their lives serves as a tangible reminder of how much you care. In this day of instant messaging and e-mails, handwritten letters are rare. If you take the time to write down your thoughts, your son or daughter will take them seriously and will have something to hold in their hands and read over and over again. You will most likely have created a treasure that they just might keep for the rest of their lives.

FROM MY HOME TO YOURS

If you don't think you are a gifted writer, please don't let that stop you. Feel free to borrow ideas from others, or to quote poetry or verses from relevant songs. Don't let anything keep you from writing what might be the single most important letter of your life! Go to a quiet place and start by writing down bullet points or the first few things that come to your mind. Create draft after draft if you need to, and if it makes you more comfortable, ask a trusted friend to review your letter for you. Or, you can ask a complete stranger—I'm more than happy to give you feedback if you would like—you can e-mail me at Rebecca.Hagelin@hotmail.com.

So what should your letter include? Here are a few thought-starters:

- **A clear statement of your love.** This doesn't have to be poetic, but it can be. However you choose to state it, your kids need to walk away from the letter knowing that you love them. Even the simple words, "I love you." written on a line all by themselves will suffice. But you must say it very clearly, one way or another. Teens today report that what they crave more than anything else in the world is to be loved. And to be blunt, if they doubt your love for them, then no matter what else you do, you have failed. (Sorry to be so harsh here.)

- **Your vision statement for their future.** Remember that vision statement you wrote? Why not share it with your child in your letter?

- **A prayer for them.** While I won't share the entire contents of the letter I wrote to my children just this past year, I will include a small sample of how I used the words of another to help me express the prayer of my heart for my children. You might even want to include this in your letter to your own kids:

This is my prayer for you:
That your love will grow more and more
That you will have knowledge and understanding with
*   your love*
That you will see the difference between good and bad
And that you will always choose the good....

Written long ago by Paul and Timothy to the Christian church in Philippi, this ancient prayer can be found in Philippians 1:9. It is so applicable to today that I can scarcely believe it was written ages ago.

I want Drew, Nick, and Kristin to love God and people more and more every day. I want them to gain knowledge, insight, and discernment on a daily basis, to build an inner compass to help them find their way, and to be so filled with understanding that they make good short and long-term decisions on their own, without my help. I want them to have the ability to always clearly see the difference between good and bad. Today's world likes to fuzz the boundaries between good and bad, between right and wrong. It's so much more confusing than even shades of gray. Mixed messages about sexual activity, respect, violence, and "tolerance" are so prevalent that today's kids are faced with a psychedelic mesh of morality where it's increasingly difficult to know where truth ends and injustice begins.

And, of course, I want their ability to do all of the above to ultimately result in their always actually choosing the good.

Isn't that what you pray for your children? If so, then tell them! Whatever it is you want them to know about you, your life, and your heart—write it down and tell them.

❏ **A warm memory you have of their childhood.** Children and teens absolutely love stories—especially about them! It excites them to know that you have a special memory of their little lives or personality stored away deep in your heart. If something doesn't come to mind right away, then just describe how you felt the first time you held them in your arms, or the smell of their little fuzzy head, or what you thought when they got on the school bus for the first time. Certainly, you can think of something!

Write a Letter to Your Teen

❏ **Positive words about them as people.** Teens today are filled with doubt about their worth, abilities, and futures. As I mention elsewhere in this book, society confuses them even more by focusing on building their "self-esteem" (See Chapter 19, "Teach Your Children Every Day That They Have God-Given Value"). What you need to do is tell them how much you think they are worth—how you value their personality, their talents, or their sense of humor. Something remarkable happens when you speak positively to a teen about them—they start giving you more of that positive attribute you have praised. When they know you think they are of value, then they start believing it.

You might also want to include the elements of the Jewish blessing that I describe in that chapter and let them know why you want to bless them every day in this manner.

❏ **Any admissions of your mistakes or failings in your relationship with them.** Ouch. This one can hurt. But your admission to your kids of your own mistakes actually creates a strong emotional bond with them—after all, if you've made a huge mistake that has hurt them, they already know it! This would be a great time to bring it out in the open and to ask for their forgiveness. It also helps them open up and ask forgiveness about their own mistakes. It's important for us to admit that we know we aren't perfect, and that we know we have a lot of work to do in order to become the parents God meant for us to be. We also need to let them know that we will keep striving to be that mom or dad that they can always count on.

❏ **A strong commitment to be there for them, regardless of the circumstances that the future may bring.** After telling them straight out that you love them, the second most powerful element of your letter will be to let them know that, as long as there is a single breath left in you, you will be there for them. Understanding what true commitment entails is something very foreign in today's world. With over half of all marriages ending in divorce, with the epidemic of absentee parents, and with the concept of "relationship" constantly portrayed only in physical sexual terms, your kids need to know that they can count on you. Regardless of how many mistakes they make, regardless of what they have done in the past, regardless of what they may do in the future, they must have someone to rely on. That person is you—and you must tell them.

IN YOUR SHOES

My pastor, Steve King, tells a beautiful story about how a very short letter from his father served to guide his conscience and actions throughout his college years:

My dad was a man of few words and did not typically write me letters—to get one from him was very unusual. When I graduated from high school and was preparing to go off to college my father penned a letter that I will always cherish. It said something like this, 'Dear Steve, Through high school you have been a fine Christian man and I am proud of you. Now that you are going off to college you will face temptations that you can not even imagine. I believe that you will remain a man of character and will face them well.' Pastor King continues, "Then my father transitioned and said, 'But even if you do not, I want you to know that I will always be on your side.'

What I explain to people is that my dad's letter kept me out of trouble in college, because my greatest fear was that I would break my father's heart."

A dear friend recently shared a letter with me that her dad wrote before she embarked on a new opportunity in her life. It reads, in part:

Dear Bek,

Thank you for your sincere love for your family. Your mother and I are so proud of you!

Your best days are ahead. Let the Word of God be on your breath. Your intoxication with his truth will lead you into opportunities and people you can never dream of. His truth will be your anchor of faith and the wisdom you need to make wise choices.

Be decisive and trust God with the results. Fear God and serve people, but keep your security wrapped up in your intimate relationship with him. Your next few months will be exciting and scary, but we are here for you.

Take time to think on quiet thoughts to balance your big dreams. Take time to do nothing, which will bring balance to your horrendous activity and sometimes torrid pace. Make sure to invest in people who can give you nothing in return to keep your motives pure and unselfish.

I love you Rebekah! Look up to your heavenly Father for his direction, look out to others for their needs, look inward to yourself for a clear conscience, and look to your family for un-

conditional love and support. Yes there are big days ahead,
but you can make every day big.
>   *Love,*
>   *Dad*

Mom, Dad, your children are hungry for your love, for your approval, and for your guidance. Please don't squander the influence and lasting impact you can have on their lives. Even if you aren't a great writer— or like my pastor's dad, are a person of few words—take the time and give the effort to write your child a letter or brief note of your commitment to them. The few minutes you invest in this project could reap a lifetime of wise choices and inspiration for generations to come.

ACT NOW

Date _____

   Today I began writing a letter to my child. I vow to complete it and give it to him/her by _____. (Set a date within the next 30 days—and stick to it!)

   _____
                        Signature

Battle The Culture,
Not Your Child

THE CHALLENGE

We all know how easy it is to get angry when we see our children make mistakes. While we cannot let children entirely off the hook and must make consistent discipline a part of our homes, we also need to realize that our kids are the targets of pernicious media, fierce advertising, and an entire army of adults who think they know how to raise our children better than we do. From the media, to educators, doctors, or child psychologists, it seems that the very institution of parenthood is under attack. And when both the mass media and adults in positions of authority degrade the basic roles of mother and father, it undermines the validity of our authority and insight with our own children.

Ending the conflict in your home starts with taking on the enemy that fired the first shots: the culture—*not* your kids.

As I pointed out in the first chapter, Commit to the Daily Battle, adults are the ones responsible for the difficult world our children must navigate.

But it's not just the adults who control the media that you need to battle. It's adults who control a growing number of professional associations such as teachers' unions and medical organizations. There was a time in this country where institutions and the adults that ran them understood that their purpose was to help parents in parenting their children—not to subvert or replace them. The schools once worked hand-in-hand with parents and encouraged parental involvement—not just activity in the PTA to help to raise money. Today, many (not all) educators believe that they actually know what is best for your son or daughter. The fact is, they can't possibly understand the history, gifts, needs, habits, dreams, and unique personality of each kid shuffled through a system built for the masses. Our children come home to *us* at night. They grow in *our* presence and we alone are equipped to look at the whole child and situation. You are the first and last defense for your child. Yet, parents often believe that we aren't smart enough to raise or educate our own kids. (Read more about this in the next chapter, "Direct Your Child's Education"). Tragically, it seems the medical community is adopting this policy more and more, too. As the health of our nation and our families have suffered due to an out of control media culture and a rejection of basic moral values, our children are paying the price. An epidemic-level number of teen pregnancies, teen sexually transmitted diseases, and a record number of kids diagnosed with clinical depression, ADD, and ADHD only encourages the government and the medical community to "step in" to take yet more control and influence away from parents. It's a maddening cycle that causes more confusion and disarray while clouding who is responsible for the inevitable increase of shattered families and damaged lives of young people. It will only become worse if parents become less relevant

I know that the constant barrage of attacks upon our children can make us feel hopeless. The battle for our children's souls is never-ending. But the good news is that we are the best ones to make a difference in our children's lives. Realizing that the battle is not with our kids is critical for parents who want to truly take back their homes.

If you try to fight the culture war in a way that creates a hostile environment, perhaps with the idea that your teen is enemy number one, you will lose the battle, and maybe even your child in the process. We must communicate to our kids that we, as their parents, are fighting *for*, not against them. We are fighting for their character, their futures, their innocence, and their childhood.

Former Colorado governor Bill Owens recently asked in a piece for The Heritage Foundation, "Does our culture truly celebrate and teach the values that made America the greatest nation on earth, or is our culture itself slowly eating away at the foundations of our nation?"

Owens writes further that the culture war "will come when parents turn off violent and hateful television shows. More important, it will come when parents teach their children how to discern the good from the bad. And it will come when we realize that we cannot abandon our children to the dark side of the Internet."

We will win when we *teach* our children rather than fight with them, when we *protect* them rather than wrestle with them, and when we assert our authority over our children rather than relinquish our roles to "the professionals."

IN YOUR SHOES

Radio and television host and commentator Laura Ingraham
included in her book *Power to the People* a story I shared with

her about my own experience in battling a professional. It was with my then-13-year-old daughter's pediatrician:

It's not just forces in the popular culture that are trying to push parents out of the way, 'health care' professionals can also step way over the line. When doctors speak, most of us listen and trust them. Then there are people like Rebecca Hagelin, author of the great book Home Invasion. A few years ago, Rebecca took her thirteen-year-old daughter Kristin to her female pediatrician (we'll call her "Dr. Smith") for a routine sports physical for her junior high track team. The doctor told Rebecca that part of the physical included a 'private chat' with Kristin.

'Excuse me?' Rebecca asked. 'What do you mean by private chat?'

'Oh, there are some things I need to talk to Kristin about and you can't be in the room,' she said matter-of-factly.

Incredulous, Rebecca shot back, 'I need to be here for any conversation you have with Kristin.'

'But you can't,' the doctor insisted. 'We're going to be talking about private things and you have to leave.'

Rebecca bristled, 'She's a minor. I'm her mother. And I will be in the room for everything.'

Dr. Smith was stunned but proceeded anyway. 'Okay, Kristin, now I'm going to have that talk with you just like I would if your mom were not here.'

She reminded Kristin that drinking was illegal until she is twenty-one and that smoking is really, really bad. Then came the money comments: 'Sex is a little trickier,' Dr. Smith said. 'You're getting to the age where girls are having boyfriends, and some of them will be kissing and doing other things. You have to do what is right for you.'

Battle the Culture, Not Your Child

At this point, Rebecca blew a gasket. 'Excuse me, but my daughter knows that sex is only for marriage.'

The good doctor looked at Rebecca in disbelief then turned to the thirteen-year-old, 'Well, that's what some people think, but you have to do what is comfortable for you.'

Parents would be disturbed to know that it is common practice among pediatricians these days to tell the moms and dads to leave the room so the 'professional' can have private chats with children—chats that involve controversial topics like abortion, premarital sex, masturbation, and birth control. Doctors think they can—and should—talk to children in a way that parents can't. It's a trend that extends from doctors' offices, to schools, to government. The 'experts' know best. Parents are too ignorant, too 'traditional,' and too incompetent to be left 'unsupervised' to direct the lives of their own children.

Good for Rebecca for saying 'back away from my child!' It's difficult to stand up to experts, doctors, and supposed authority figures. And too many parents just take it. Think about what that approach communicates to your child.

Of course, that was the last time I went back to that doctor! I still shudder when I think about it. The doctor obviously didn't expect to get my push-back anymore than I expected her to challenge me on my own authority with my daughter. But you as a mom or dad must push back! On the way home in the car that day I had the following conversation with Kristin:

'Kristin, do you know what just happened in there? That doctor tried to drive a wedge between us. She tried to isolate you from me, and pass on her own values to you.' Kristin replied, 'I know, Mom. And I know why you are upset.'

"Good," I responded. "Because I want you to know that if something bad were to happen to you, it's not the doctor that will be there for you. It's me. It's me and your dad that will always be there for you. She might be a "professional" but she's not your mom. She is a bystander who doesn't know or love you—she's already on to the next patient by now. Your dad and I love you more than anyone else in the world possibly could. And we know what's best for you. And I refuse to let anyone interfere with my commitment to you, or with my ability to protect and teach you.

Kristin got it, and she still recalls the power of the way I rose up like a mother bear to swat down anyone who might lead her astray. Guess what? My bond with my daughter was actually strengthened that day. We won that battle over the adult who tried to impose *her* worldview on my precious child. It took courage, and discomfort, but we did it. And you can, too.

FROM MY HOME TO YOURS

In addition to making it clear that you are the authority figure in your child's life, here are other ways you can fight the culture war without fighting your kids:

❏ **Remind your child of who you are.** Regardless of what our children might tell us, they long to know that we are in control. The last thing they want is to be shoved around between adults, manipulated by *anyone*, or led to believe that everything is relative. Teens are looking for boundaries, for a firm foundation they can count on, for solid advice, and for someone who can be responsible for them.

They are looking for someone to believe in. Remind them through conversation and actions that you are that person. (See Chapter 12, "Learn How to Have Meaningful Discussions With Your Child.")

❏ **Assert your authority with other adults.** (I just can't say this enough.) My goodness, it seems that nearly every day I have to remind other adults that I am my child's parent, and that they have no right to instruct or advise them without my permission! It's not the teacher, it's not the doctor, and it's not the social worker that will be held accountable if your child gets in trouble. It is YOU.

❏ **Interact with local media.** When you see something pernicious aimed at your child by a local radio or television outlet, call the station manager and follow-up with a letter demanding a reply. Write an op-ed for your weekly newspaper, or a letter to the editor for your daily paper. You can find out how to do this by reading the editorial page. Papers have rules for opinion pieces and letters they may publish. You must follow them if you want to see your piece in print. You may be surprised to find that you are voicing what lots of other parents are feeling! (See Chapter 13, "Secure Allies in the Battle.")

❏ **Organize a group of parents to visit the teacher.** If you have issues with the way a teacher or school handles something, like sex education in the classroom, for example, chances are that other parents feel the same way. Remember that the schools exist to help you teach your children, not to dictate their brand of morality. You have an absolute right to express your concerns, and if other parents do it too, you will have a better chance of a positive outcome. But, above all else, be kind and respectful, and only take kind and respectful parents with you. Make sure that if you point out a problem, you also offer a solution that would apply to your child and the children of those who believe as you do. You are not there to force your beliefs on other students any more than you would expect other parents to force their beliefs on your child. But you do have an absolute right to make certain that your faith and moral beliefs are not trampled by the public school that you are paying for.

❑ **Organize boycotts with other parents.** Again, there is strength in numbers. You'd be amazed at how quickly a local business will respond to requests from customers and potential customers in their neighborhood. And you'll also probably be surprised by how many willing participants are out there. A survey of women by the Motherhood Project revealed that most moms wish that parents would join forces in fighting the adults who seek to manipulate our kids. Even a short letter with twenty signatures of parents who share your concerns can get a local merchant to remove a product or stop an inappropriate marketing campaign aimed at your child. Just remember to be nice, but firm. And if the owner does respond positively, reward him by shopping at his business in the future and encouraging others to do the same.

❑ **Form a blog with other parents.** You can also join an already established blog about tools and tips in fighting back against greedy advertising and the pop-culture onslaught.

❑ **Write to the CEOs and board members of companies negatively targeting your child.** Odds are, you'll catch the attention of at least one empathetic parent who serves on the board, or one executive who doesn't want angry parents denting quarterly earnings.

Battle the Culture, Not Your Child

MORE HELP

■ Dr. Bill Maier of Focus on the Family is one of the leading experts on how you can battle the culture and, in so doing, actually cause your kids to love you more. One particular book he edited, *Help! My Teen Thinks I'm the Enemy* explains, "Your teen really does want a good relationship with you, though at times it may feel like you're enduring the Cold War. [This] can help you build a strong and lasting relationship with your child, through the teen years and beyond." You can order this great resource and others by Dr. Maier at family.org. Dr. Maier knows what he is talking about and should be one of your first resources.

■ *So sexy, So soon: The New Sexualized Childhood and What Parents Can Do to Protect Their Kids* is a super book filled with great ideas on how to battle the culture. Written by Diane Levin and Jeanne Kilbourne, it is filled with tips and stories of success to equip and encourage you.

continued

MORE HELP

■ *Culture Warrior* by Bill O'Reilly. Bill covers the battleground for our culture by outlining a number of issues and decrying the erosion of societal discipline.

■ *Power to the People*, by Laura Ingraham. Laura's book explains your rights as both a parent and a citizen in a powerful handbook on how to stop the creep of influence that undermines your authority.

■ The website of the American Family Association (afa.net) has a great section called "Activism" where you can get tips on how to approach businesses when you feel they are degrading community standards. You can find out how to fight raunchy billboards, and other marketing campaigns that corrupt decency.

■ Citizens for Community Values (cvv.org) also runs a terrific site that shows you the difference you can make, and provides you with the tools to do it. The organization's mission is to *"promote Judeo-Christian moral values, and to reduce destructive behaviors contrary to those values, through education, active community partnership, and individual empowerment at the local, state and national levels."* Their site is chock full of ways you can make a difference.

Direct Your
Child's Education

THE CHALLENGE

With "free" education offered in every town in the United States, a plethora of teachers who seem to be more than willing to take a role of authority in place of parents, and the convenience of sending our children to someone else to educate them, many parents have relinquished their role as the primary director of their children's education. Our kids spend more awake time in schoolrooms during their formative years than just about any place else other than home. But it seems that most parents don't have a clue what their children are being taught.

Even the most expensive private school can be a moral wasteland. Although a high price tag might indicate academic excellence, it can also reflect that the school may contain a level of intellectual snobbery or an air of superiority that assumes that faith in God and traditional moral values are foolishness. Conversely, many nurturing religious schools lack an emphasis on academic achievement. The bottom line is, you have to do your own homework before you can be certain that the private schools in your area are all that you hope for. Don't get me wrong—with the growing failures of the public schools, there has been a rise in the number of private schools across the nation that can help our children to excel both spiritually and academically. You just have to find out what is available to you.

Of course, everyone knows—though few want to face it—that the performance level of the public school system is dismal. Study after study show that American public education is failing when compared to the rest of the civilized world. According to The Heritage Foundation, "Standardized test scores in verbal and mathematics aptitude have declined steadily over the past 19 years." The Heritage report goes on to say, "Naturally, the hard disciplines of physics, chemistry, engineering, and mathematics have suffered, with possible disastrous impact on the U.S. ability to compete on the world market."

Add to that the rampant behavioral problems, and sexually explicit "family life education" materials that often teach our kids that they are expected to have sex as teens, and you've got a host of reasons not to send your children to public school.

This chapter is not meant to bash you if your children are in a public school setting. My own children have attended our local public high schools and at the writing of this book, my daughter is still a student there. The reality is, however, you must be diligent about finding out what goes on in the classroom, what your kids are reading, and whether your values are under attack. If you have the slightest indication that your child is susceptible to manipulation or may be influenced by the lack of morality on display in the government schools, then I strongly urge you to look for other educational options. If you determine that your child should attend public schools, then I hope to help you begin to navigate those treacherous waters and encourage you to maximize your parental rights. Warning: this chapter only scratches the surface of how you can affect what goes on in the classroom. It is not meant to be an all-encompassing, fool-proof method for your situation. It is intended, however, to encourage you to take control of your child's education by becoming an active participant. Your commitment in taking on that responsibility is the first, and most important, of the *many* steps you will need to make over the years.

It's time to take an active role in your child's education. Read their textbooks, interact with their teachers, understand your rights as a parent, question materials, and never, ever assume that someone knows how to teach your child better than you do.

The Heritage Foundation reports that parental involvement emerges as a "robust influence on educational outcomes. It is multidimensional. Ways to be involved include monitoring children's activities outside home and school; setting rules; having conversations about and helping children with school work and school-related issues; holding high educational expectations; discussing future planning with children and helping them with important decision making; participating in school-related activities such as meeting with teachers and volunteering in the classroom; and reading to children or engaging in other enrichment or leisure activities together."

Heritage Foundation education expert, Christine Kim, further reports:

> While academic research has consistently shown that increased spending does not correlate with educational gains, the research does show a strong relationship between parental influences and children's educational outcomes, from school readiness to college completion. Two compelling parental factors emerge:

1. family structure, i.e., the number of parents living in the student's home and their relationships to the child, and
2. parents' involvement in their children's schoolwork.

Consequently, the solution to improving educational outcomes begins at home, by strengthening marriage and promoting stable family formation and parental involvement.

FROM MY HOME TO YOURS

Evaluate each of your children's needs and your academic choices: I'm the mom of three, and I know from experience that my children are not cookie-cutter images of each other. They have different academic strengths and weaknesses, different tolerance levels, and very different personalities. And they have not maintained the exact levels of interest and needs over the years. Different children have different ways of learning, and it's up to me—not some educator who can't possibly know or love them like I do—to make the decisions about how and where they should learn. Every parent should have the choice and freedom to select the educational setting that is best for each of their children.

We've educated our three children in virtually every possible setting over the years—home school, private school and public schools. My husband and I determined long ago that our family will march to the beat of our own drummer. We refuse to be victims of snobbery by those parents who insist that private schools are the best. We won't allow ourselves to be shamed by well-meaning parents who insist that if we don't home school then we are less committed to our kids than they are to theirs. And we absolutely reject *both* the conventional wisdom that public education is the answer, and the notion that all public schools are failing schools. We have never forced all of our children into one educational mold out of a desire for convenience. It makes life a little more complicated to actually have to evaluate what situations are best for your kids, but it is absolutely worth it.

SERIOUSLY CONSIDER EVERY OPTION—INCLUDING HOME SCHOOLING. Research the schools in your area. What are the test scores? What are the behavior problems? How are students disciplined? How much parental involvement is allowed? What textbooks are used? Is abstinence education the basis for "sex ed"—or something else? The bottom line is that if a school is keeping you in the dark about materials, classroom procedures, or personal involvement, then they probably have an agenda they are hiding. It might be academic content that emerges as the problem—or it might be an attitude of superiority that seeks to keep you effectively locked out of your child's education. In either case, I have one piece of advice: *Grab your kids and run for their lives!* If an adult in "authority" ever tries to force their brand of morality on your children, if any system that has your sons or daughters in their care says that you as the parent don't belong, then just *get up and go.*

There is a huge body of research that proves that home schooled children as a whole soar over their peers academically, psychologically and socially. The website of The Home School Legal Defense Association (hslda.org) has a compilation of studies from around the nation that show how the individual attention and atmosphere that home schooled children receive is superior to a system of mass education. Here is but a sampling of that research:

> In 1997, a study of 5,402 home school students from 1,657 families was released. It was entitled, "Strengths of Their Own: Home Schoolers Across America." The study demonstrated that home schoolers, on the average, out-performed their counterparts in the public schools by 30 to 37 percentile points in all subjects. A significant finding when analyzing the data for 8th

graders was the evidence that home schoolers who are home schooled two or more years score substantially higher than students who have been home schooled one year or less. The new home schoolers were scoring on the average in the 59th percentile compared to students home schooled the last two or more years who scored between 86th and 92nd percentile.

This was confirmed in another study by Dr. Lawrence Rudner of 20,760 home schooled students which found the home schoolers who have home schooled all their school aged years had the highest academic achievement. This was especially apparent in the higher grades. This is a good encouragement to families to catch the long-range vision and home school through high school.

Another important finding of Strengths of Their Own was that the race of the student does not make any difference. There was no significant difference between minority and white home schooled students. For example, in grades K–12, both white and minority students scored, on the average, in the 87th percentile. In math, whites scored in the 82nd percentile while minorities scored in the 77th percentile. In the public schools, however, there is a sharp contrast. White public school eighth grade students, nationally scored the 58th percentile in math and the 57th percentile in reading. Black eighth grade students, on the other hand, scored on the average at the 24th percentile in math and the 28th percentile in reading. Hispanics scored at the 29th percentile in math and the 28th percentile in reading.

If you decide it is time to take full control of your kids' education, know that home schooling isn't what the mass media would have you believe it is. And the name, "home schooling" is actually a misnomer—much of it is now done through co-ops, by hiring tutors skilled in a specific area, in group settings with others, and online through acclaimed institutions. Given all the support and technology available to parents today, you just might be surprised to find that home schooling is right for you and your children.

VIGILANCE IS THE KEY TO SUCCESS. No matter which settings you choose for your children, your eternal vigilance must be present if you are to succeed in developing your child's emotional, intellectual, and spiritual abilities to their fullest. Hands-on interaction is critical. If you find something offensive or incorrect in their textbooks, challenge it with the teacher. Volunteer during school hours so you can see what is really going on. Know your rights—such as opting your child out of sex education/family life classes. As a matter of fact, exploring the content of the sex education materials in your child's school should be a priority for you.

These classes often start in grade school and set the stage for an entire worldview that may be contrary to yours. Go to the school today and find out the content of the curriculum—my guess is, you will want to opt your child out. If you don't like what you see or how you are treated, please e-mail me at Rebecca.Hagelin@hotmail.com. I am so concerned about the content of these classes that I pledge to connect you with someone who can help you figure out what to do to keep your child from being indoctrinated. You should also alert others who share your concerns and beliefs and work together to find solutions that fit your particular situation.

IN YOUR SHOES

Since the vast majority of children in the United States are educated in public schools at some time in their lives, I thought it was important to share inspiring stories from parents who have refused to relinquish their parental control or beliefs in such settings. My public education hero is a man whom I have never met. But he shared his story with me via e-mail how he worked with the system in order to protect his family's intellectual and faith beliefs. Gary wrote:

When our son was in grade school, we received a call from the teacher explaining that he had been disruptive in class. He had challenged the teacher during a science lesson and said she was wrong when stating that the earth is billions of years old. He would not back down, so she escorted him to the office. I also knew this teacher had a Masters in Geology, so I prayed really hard that night.

When I met with her I was humble and had my son repeat what had occurred. He also stated "But that's what YOU told me, Dad!" I agreed and she added "I understand your religious beliefs say one thing, but science shows us otherwise."

I politely disagreed, saying science really is not able to state such, and gave her a couple of video tapes including "Young Age" and Mt. St. Helens by the Institute for Creation Research and "The Secret of Dinosaurs" by Master Books, as well as some technical articles from True Origins. We had a very polite and agreeable half hour meeting.

I never attacked her or railed about Evolution/Indoctrination/Secularism but treated her like I would like to be treated.

At the end of this she shocked me by saying "Perhaps for now instead of saying Billions or Millions of years instead just say "really ancient."

I added, "Yes, some of these kids might think their grandparents are ancient.'

She laughed at that and thanked me for staying understanding and polite, as she had been confronted before by

other parents and was dreading another 'angry confrontation'.
She was truly impressed with the reasons I presented to help
her see the other side of this debate.

Gary also wrote that this same teacher later invited him to give a presentation before her class and said, "She still held to Evolution, but for the rest of the school year presented both sides whenever she talked over anything about Origins or evolution of life issues. In fact she even showed some of the videos to her class and to other teachers so they could become more aware of this "controversy." Gary is a wonderful example of how it is possible to influence the teacher if you come equipped with information and the right attitude.

Most teachers teach because they love children and knowledge. But others have an agenda and can even trample on your rights or practice intimidation if you let them. It is absolutely essential that you never allow the public schools to infringe on the religious beliefs that you are trying to pass on to your children, or deny your child the right to express free speech. I have listed legal organizations in the More Help section that provide free services to families who have had their Constitutional rights infringed. They don't accept every case, but they will hear you out and offer thoughtful, sound advice on how to handle your situation.

Another reader named Michael describes his successes in asserting parental authority over two non-academic activities that take place in many schools:

When my son was in sixth grade, his class was having a
"movie" day. The children were asked to bring in movies and

the class would watch them. No biggie, right? I was expecting cartoons and such. But the teacher selected 'Friday the 13th'! My son told the teacher that he was not allowed to watch "R" rated movies and asked to be excused to go to the library. The teacher told him no. So he went to the principal and told her what was going on. She called my wife, who picked him up and they spent the day together. When I got home and was informed of the goings-on, I called the principal at home and threatened a law suit if that teacher was not disciplined in some manner. The woman came to our house the next day after school and apologized, and admitted that she had erred. It sufficed for us.

When our oldest daughter was in middle school, her class was planning an overnight trip to nearby Chicago to include museums and shopping and such. Our daughter wanted to go and she wanted her mother to go along as a chaperone. We filled out all the paperwork and paid the fees, etc. The week before the trip was to occur, the school counselor called and said that parents would not be allowed to go, something about the Insurance not covering them. We asked how many female chaperones there would be. The answer was two—for over thirty young ladies! We told her, and the principal, that they were "stoned" if they thought two was enough, and no, our daughter (and her best friend) would not be going. So, instead of a class field trip, my wife took our daughter and her friend (with her mother's consent) on a field trip that involved figuring out bus and train routes, fares, etc. They rode trains and buses, went to the Field Museum in downtown Chicago, shopped, and had an absolutely great time. My daughter, who now has three of her own children, still remarks fondly upon that day.

Direct Your Child's Education

ACT NOW

Date _____

Today I pledged to direct my child's education. I began to evaluate each of my children and their needs in order to determine what is best for them and our family.

_____

Signature

MORE HELP

If you believe you or your child's constitutional rights have been denied by your local public school, these organizations provide free advice and in some cases, legal action. The best bet is to contact them through their websites:

Alliance Defense Fund (AllianceDefenseFund.org)

American Center for Law and Justice (ACLJ.org)

The Rutherford Institute (rutherford.org)

If you home school and believe that you are being denied your rights, the Home School Legal Defense Association (hslda.org) can help. You should also visit and join the parent organization, the Home School Foundation, because they offer practical advice on everything from curriculum, to teaching tips, to support groups in your area. Both organizations were founded by Mike Farris, the guru of the modern home schooling movement, and membership in them is a "must" for any family who has taken complete control of their child's education. I just can't say enough good things about their resources, conferences, website, and camaraderie. They even have real help for single parents and the parents of disabled children who want to home school their kids. Your portal to all of these services is hsf.org.

Learn How To Have Meaningful Discussions With Your Child

THE CHALLENGE

Do you ever feel like talking to your child is like talking to a wall? Does it seem like things go in one ear and out the other? Or, do you ever feel like every time you say something to your child, a fireworks display of emotion is likely to ensue?

You are not alone. Learning the art of meaningful discussion with your child can be the hardest part of being a parent. Engaging your child without talking down to him, or talking at a level too complex for her to grasp, is truly an art, and getting your children to feel comfortable talking to you about their joys or concerns is challenging. Finding the balance in being a friend as well as a disciplinarian may sometimes seem nearly impossible.

The very nature of conversation requires it to be two-way. If one person is blah, blah, blahing, and the other is sulking nearby on the couch, arms folded and rolling his eyes, then it's not a discussion. It just doesn't count. Believe me, as a mother of three, I've had those "chats" before and they usually don't end well.

Having meaningful conversations with your child is critical to developing a strong relationship that will last into adulthood. Such chats can also help keep your children safe and teach them values and principles that will protect their futures.

An article published in *Adolescence* in 2002 reported, "Considerable research has been devoted to forms of communication between parents and children. Several studies have reported that youth from families with frequent, open (bidirectional), and positive communication are less likely to become involved with drugs. These youth are also more likely to have abstinence-based norms than are youth from families in which this kind of dialogue is absent."

The article continues to argue, "Discussions that involve both children's and parents' perspectives have been found to promote the development of conventional standards of conduct."

There is an undeniable direct and positive correlation between learning how to reach your child in a discussion and how they will do in their future.

IN YOUR SHOES

The following story, sent to me by Ana, describes a few ways to get the conversation process rolling. She writes:

When I turned fifteen, communication with my mother began to break down. Talking about the tough issues that typically arise during the teenage years devolved into regular fights, ending usually with tears and yelling. When I wanted to see a movie my mother did not agree on or wear a swimsuit that she did not approve of, a war of words was bound to ensue.

We essentially stopped discussing things. Instead, we would fight, argue, talk over each other's heads, yell, slam doors, and cry.

It did not take long for both of us to realize that it had to stop.

We did two things to work towards solving the problem.

First, we formed a discussion group with my three closest girlfriends and their mothers. We selected readings that walked through many of the common struggles between parents and teenagers, such as clothing and dating. The books covered numerous topics with discussion questions and real-life stories, some modern, some biblical.

Our group began meeting every other week, each daughter taking turns selecting a fun coffee-shop or restaurant. For the first forty-five minutes of our get-together, we would socialize, laugh, and have a good time. After we were all feeling comfortable and in good spirits, we would begin our discussions. It could not have been a more healthy experience. For the girls, it provided an open and fun forum for expressing our feelings on "hot topics." For our mothers, they got the chance to express their concerns. We got to hear about their own life experiences, their own regrets in dating, dressing, and other choices they wanted to share. The conversations remained under control because no one wanted to cry or yell in front of everyone else. And the best part, we got to laugh through it all. We formed bonds with each other and learned what meaningful and positive discussion about hard issues can look like. We read about women who have gone before us and been faced with making hard ethical choices.

The ice began to thaw with my mother as we both had an outlet for positive expression and dialogue.

The second thing that we did was write contracts together for issues that we were fighting about. We regularly fought about how clean I had to keep my room. She felt like it had to be spic and span; I couldn't understand why I could not have privacy and some leeway to make choices about how I lived. Clothes on my floor were not hurting anyone after all!

After one tear-filled fight that ensued when I was grounded for leaving out some clothes, we decided to sit down and work through a plan. I wrote out what I thought was a fair standard for room cleanliness and privacy and she wrote out her version. We then, with my Dad acting as a moderator, worked out a final standard that was a compromise between our two ideals, got it in writing, and then signed it.

We never fought about the cleanliness of my room again. But better yet, we learned something about a great way to have a meaningful discussion about a topic causing us strife, and a potential way to resolve it.

Writing a contract is probably not the best way for everyone to work out a problem. But having both sides put their thoughts in writing is a great way to getting a meaningful conversation off to a good start.

The way you talk to your child may end up being unique to your relationship. When I was a pre-teen, my mother developed a very unusual but effective way to talk to me about difficult issues. She would offer to wash my hair—no kidding. I would stand at the bathroom counter and lean over and put my head in the sink. Mom would usually use a cup to drench my hair with warm water and then soap up my head and the "discussion" would begin. It sounds odd, but I was actually comforted by the process. For me, it was a matter of being re-moved from the glare of an interrogation light—because in reality, I was under a spigot. No one was watching my expression, there was no eye contact, and it didn't matter if I cried—my face was wet any-way. She would always gently massage my head and say positive words of encouragement. But if there had been an issue or concern or big life "fact" she needed to tell me, you can sure bet I heard it even through any water in my ears.

FROM MY HOME TO YOURS

As a mother, I've always tried to keep my eyes open in search of an op-portunity to communicate with my kids. Here are a few tips I learned along the way:

- ❑ **Make yourself available.** When your kids are home, do whatever you can to be home, too. I've spent many an evening just relaxing on the sofa when I know they are going to be hanging out. The kitchen is also a good place to plant myself on a weekend—hungry teens in search of food will enter sooner or later and, most likely, a com-fortable opportunity to converse will usually present it-self.
- ❑ **Always offer to drive the masses.** Ok, so this one sounds nuts. But as often as possible, I offer to be the driver when my children and their friends are headed out. It's so much fun to listen to childhood and teen banter—and almost miraculously, when lots of bodies are in the car, you become a natural part of conversation and laughter.
- ❑ **Drive your child to school for as long as you can.** My husband always made a point to drive our kids to school in

the mornings whenever he could. He found that our daughter was willing to start the day out with dad despite her often sleepy disposition, because it meant she didn't have to ride the school bus! Now that she's old enough to drive herself, she truly treasures all those early mornings when it was just her and dad in the car. And my husband treasures them, too. The rides were short but she got the message loud and clear that dad was always there, ready and willing to chat. Even though she didn't usually choose to take advantage of the conversation opportunity, she always knew she could if she wanted to. And that made a huge difference.

❏ **Turn off the television when eating meals.** I wish this was more obvious than it seems to be. Surveys show that over half of teens say their parents keep the television on when having family dinners—which don't happen very often to begin with. Having the boob tube on means an opportunity for conversation is lost forever.

❏ **Initiate, initiate, initiate.** Did I make my point? Kids often feel a bit awkward about broaching a difficult subject. You're the parent—part of your job is to take the initiative and teach them how to communicate. Be sensitive to their moods and the conditions. Actively look for opportunities to engage them in meaningful conversations. If your normally hyper-active teen son is unusually pensive, sit by his side and find out what is going on in his head. If your child walks in the door joyous, for goodness sake, put down what you are doing and find out the source of her joy so you can share in it! And always end every conversation with a positive and encouraging comment—then seal it with a quick hug or some other physical contact such as a squeeze of the hand or a pat on the back.

Learn How to Have Meaningful Discussions...

Another key to developing a habit of significant discussions with your child is learning his or her own special way of communicating. Gary Chapman writes in his renowned book, *The Five Love Languages*, "each child develops unique emotional patterns." He argues that most people communicate and feel love in one or two predominant languages: quality time, words of affirmation, gifts, acts of services, and physical touch. Chapman urges parents to spend time observing their children. How do they communicate? Do they ask to spend special time alone with you? Do they run up and give you hugs? Do they quietly do a chore without being asked? Looking for these cues can help you speak to your child on a very deep and intimate level. Knowing their special way of communicating can help you to reach out to them and begin meaningful discussions in a way that speaks to them deeply.

ACT NOW

Date _____

Today I let my children know that I want to hear more of what they have to say, and to be available to share more openly with them.

I initiated meaningful conversation with_____about _____on _____(date).

_____
Signature

MORE HELP

Doug Phillips, who runs the best catalogue of parenting resources I know about—"Reformation and Revival—The Vision Forum Family Catalogue"— offers a very special series for fathers entitled, "How to Talk to Your Sons About the Hard Things." The six-part DVD series, by Geoffrey Botkin and his five sons, features real-life conversations that will inspire you to talk more to your sons. The series is also available at visionforum.com

Vision Forum also offers, *Raising Maidens of Virtue* to help parents discuss sensitive issues with their daughters. This book, by Stacy McDonald, is designed for parents of daughters of all ages.

Family.org, a website of Focus on the Family, contains numerous resources on how to improve communications with your children and others. I encourage you to curl up in a comfy chair with your laptop and favorite beverage and log on to family.org—you might just be there for hours!

Vow To Be The Parent (Not Your Child's Best Friend)

THE CHALLENGE

It's one of the first words children learn to say: "No." Yet no matter how much their offspring misbehave, many parents can't seem to bear using it themselves.

Maybe these permissive mothers and fathers are too tired after a long day at work to stand their ground. Perhaps they're so accustomed to dealing with other adults that compromise has become second nature to them. Whatever the reason, I can tell you this: these doormats are doing their children—not to mention themselves and the rest of society—no favors. As night follows day, their selfish, unhappy tots are going to grow into selfish, unhappy teenagers.

That's one more unfortunate result of our politically correct culture. We've swung from the old Victorian extreme ("children are to be seen, not heard") to another ("children are to be catered to, lest you bruise their fragile egos.") Look at all the books and magazines on child-rearing that focus only on the short-term goal of getting past one particular battle. They recommend various ways to distract your child or bargain with him. In short, *anything* to avoid saying, "No." Never mind that, by not acting like the parent, you've abdicated crucial ground in the larger effort to raise a thoughtful, well-behaved, independent teen who will go on to become a responsible adult.

Of course, it could be that the publishers of these books and magazines know their audience—and its hunger for pat answers. "We want guarantees," writes syndicated columnist Betsy Hart in her book, *It Takes a Parent.* "But the only thing we really know is that we have a duty as parents to persevere. And in that perseverance lies the best hope for our children."

As a mother of three, I can truly appreciate her point. Most parents have solid instincts about what's right and wrong, and they have a pretty good sense of how to raise their children to understand one from the other. Parents make mistakes—but we can learn from them. The trick is in sticking with it, day after day, for years.

But stick with it we must. Why? Because we love our children—even when they're acting unlovable. And because, as Hart puts it in a theme that recurs throughout her book, "we need to be on a rescue mission for our children's hearts." The reason is simple: What we do is a reflection of our character. If we persevere in planting good virtues in our children—and we do that by being their *parents*, not their friends—we won't have to worry so much about how they will behave under pressure. (Of course, we'll never stop worrying altogether—we *are* parents, after all.)

Consider two people that Hart uses as examples to show that "training can take over when it comes to the heart": Bruce Ismay and

Vow to Be the Parent (Not Your Child's Best Friend)

Todd Beamer. Ismay was president of the White Star Line, which produced the Titanic, and was on the ship when it sank. But unlike hundreds of his passengers, he survived. Why? Because, Hart says, he was able to board a lifeboat "ahead of other potential male passengers because of his status." Contrast that with Todd Beamer, who was on United Airlines Flight 93 on September 11, 2001. When it became apparent that terrorists were using the plane for a suicide mission, Beamer rallied his fellow passengers to stop their attackers. We know the result. Instead of slamming into the U.S. Capitol or a similar target, the plane crashed into a Pennsylvania field.

Was Bruce Ismay a born coward and was Todd Beamer a born hero? No. But in a moment of supreme peril, both showed their true character. Vice and virtue had no doubt been reinforced time and again during their lifetimes. When the Big Moment came, each acted accordingly. A hero, let's remember, acts unselfishly—and that's the kind of character trait that develops when parents take the time and the trouble to "be the parent." It's hard, of course. But as the saying goes, nothing really worthwhile is ever easy. There will be a few tears here and there, even some hurt feelings from time to time, but, believe it or not, the sky won't fall.

In fact, on some level, your children will appreciate it. They may not admit it, but deep down, they're longing for guidance and for boundaries. Some interesting public-service announcements that aired a few years ago made this point nicely. They depicted several different older teenagers, each telling the viewer how upset he was when his parents said no to staying out too late, to hanging with the wrong crowd, or to doing drugs. The message is loud and clear. They were angry that their parents didn't give in. But at the end, they look into the camera, pause, and say: "Thanks."

Yes, in retrospect they appreciate what their parents did. They realize, years after the fact, that it was done out of love (although you can be sure they were convinced at the time that their parents "hated" them). And that's the point. You're the adult—it's your job to look down that road and do what it takes to ensure their future happiness. And that means acting like a parent.

Having the guts to say "no" when appropriate is also a good way to save your children from the "anything-goes" culture that surrounds us. Modern parents seem to enthrone their children and constantly reinforce the notion that the world revolves around them. In the process, they create monsters who are a terror not only to others but to themselves, if the rising rates of depression are any indication.

These spoiled children are filled with false self-esteem (See "Teach Your Children Every Day That They Have God-Diven Value") and have no real sense that personal dignity comes with treating others as you would like to be treated (See "Let the Golden Rule, Rule Your Home").

You have authority simply because you are a parent. God didn't give children to children—he gave them to parents. They need us to guide and direct them with the experience that comes from the school of hard knocks and from a position of authority. Your child needs you to be his mom or dad—not just another drifting peer trying to figure out your way in the world.

FROM MY HOME TO YOURS:

❑ **Set clear boundaries.** Take something like non-homework computer time. Teens need to know how much of it they're allowed to have. A vaguely worded caution, such as "Don't be on there too long"—followed by irritation when they've passed some time marker that's only in your own head—doesn't help. Tell them clearly, you can only be online for x minutes—and stick to it. The same principle applies to other areas of life. Let them know, as clearly as possible, what you expect.

Vow to Be the Parent (Not Your Child's Best Friend)

❏ **Enforce the rules.** Rules without enforcement are mean-ingless. Yet we constantly hear parents saying "don't do that" again and again—as the child, of course, does it re-peatedly with no consequences. It would actually be bet-ter for these parents to say nothing and let their kids simply do whatever they wanted. That way, at least, the parents wouldn't be teaching their children contempt for authority.

❏ **Don't plead with your children to behave.** Make it clear that you expect them to obey. Obedience is a dirty word in our pop culture. But if you don't require it with your kids, you will all be in trouble. You will set them up for failure in life now and in the future. Teens have to obey the rules at school or they could get suspended; teens and adults have to obey the rules of the workplace or they could get fired, and so on. As a parent, teaching your children or teens to obey means (brace yourself, modern parents) say-ing a well-considered "no" and remaining firm. Despite what many parenting "experts" will say, your child won't be scarred for life. Indeed, he'll be much better off. If you really love him, you're more concerned with shaping his character and teaching him how to succeed in life than you are with winning a popularity contest. Let's face it: there's no other reason to *bother* being the parent—because set-ting rules and enforcing them means hard work. Nothing could be easier than just sitting back and letting our chil-dren become tyrants. We do the work of being parents be-cause we love our children.

❏ **Don't discipline in anger.** I know—easier said than done. We've all had moments when we've flown off the handle and reacted in anger. But it's important for your children to realize that their punishment is just, and that it's not coming simply because you're upset. Take some time to cool off before you say or do something you might regret. There's nothing wrong with saying, "We'll talk about this later, young man." (Make sure you do, of course!)

❏ **Find a mentor—for you.** Many of you reading this book have come from less than perfect homes. You may have horrible memories of your mother and father, or you may have no memories of them at all—because they weren't there. Regardless of your circumstances and heartache, you can become the parent of your child's dreams. Mentors are important for people of all ages—especially for parents who are single, struggling, or have bad childhood memories of their own. Moms, find an older, respected mother in your church or community, and let her know you would like to learn from her. Dads, seek out grandfathers and older men of strong moral character to help you succeed at being a loving father. The point is, you don't have to make it up or do it alone. Get help, and in turn, your interest can bless the one who is mentoring you. (See the next chapter, "Secure Allies in the Battle" for more tips.)

IN YOUR SHOES

When I encouraged readers of my *Townhall* column to submit their stories for this book, I received insight, wisdom, and encouragement and have shared much of it with you. This letter, from a woman who only wanted to be identified as L.C., is a poignant reminder of just how desperately our children want us to truly parent them. I share it for two reasons: 1) to remind you that you have the power to shape your child forever, and,

Vow to Be the Parent (Not Your Child's Best Friend)

2) to comfort you if you grew up in a home with a parent who was hurtful. God offers healing for those who suffer from negligent parenting—and part of that healing can come from becoming the parent to your kids you always dreamed of having.

Mrs. Hagelin,

I've read your columns ever since I discovered Townhall.com, and I loved Home Invasion. I wrote today because everyone should know how important it is for parents to be parents.

In high school, I would hear girls complain about how their parents were too strict; some would change into clothes that showed noticeably more skin once they got to school, complaining that their parents wouldn't let them out the door if they knew that's what she was wearing that day. Sometimes I couldn't stay silent any more and I would say, "You really don't know how blessed you are." You see, I was one of the girls who didn't have that, and I suffered for it.

My mom was absent for most of my childhood, and the times when she was there were characterized by extreme dysfunction more than anything else. She would buy and encourage me to wear the short little skirts, then turn around and tell me that I looked like a hooker the next day when she changed her mind about them. The one thing I wanted growing up was a clear standard. One moment my mom wanted to be my friend instead of my mom, the next she was a completely unreasonable authoritarian. I never knew where I stood with her. God heals a lot of scars, and today I'm 22 years old and in grad school, but I still yearn for that guidance that I know I'll never have from her.

Please keep up the good work; I hope many children will grow up not knowing how blessed they are to have good *parents, because the only ones who know what a blessing it is are too often the ones who never had it.*

    God bless,

    L.C.

ACT NOW

Date _____

    Today I began being the parent in my home. I pledge to give my children the boundaries and discipline they need—and in so doing, to show the depth of my love for them.

_____

                  Signature

Vow to Be the Parent (Not Your Child's Best Friend)

Secure Allies
In The Battle

THE CHALLENGE

Fighting the culture and seemingly everything in it can be a lonely battle. Of course, the trick of a formidable enemy is to make you think you are the only one– it's a classic tactic to make you want to give-up, give-in, or run away!

At first you might actually seem like the only one—you've probably heard it from your kids a thousand times if you've even slightly ventured into the culture war. "You're the *only mom* that won't let her kid go to that movie"—"You're the *only dad* that won't let his son play that video game"—"You're the *only parents* that want to talk to the teacher."

If you've heard these words, your child just might have an unintended but important point—why are you the *"only one"*—the only parent—your child knows who has your values? Isn't up to you to find other adults who do? Taking time to secure allies who share your worldview will not only make life easier for you, it will make it far easier for your child. No teen wants to feel isolated, left out, and "weird." The reality is, there are probably many more parents who share your concerns than you realize—but they, too, may have not dared to venture out and ask for help.

A Gallup poll revealed that 82 percent of Republicans and 78 percent of Democrats believe that American values today are fair to downright poor because of the pop culture. In another study, 2,000 mothers were interviewed by researchers at the University of Minnesota on behalf of the Motherhood Project. The women were from all walks of life and included both moms who work outside the home and those who work inside the home. They were from many different socio-economic classes and various races. Yet they all shared the common worry about the harmful effects the modern culture is having on America's kids. The good news here is, although the world would have you feel ostracized for your concerns, you are in good company. There is a silent army—probably many in your sphere of influence—who are looking for leadership and reinforcement in fighting the cultural battle!

We weren't meant to do this alone—to face the world by ourselves with our families standing vulnerable against the onslaught of a toxic culture. There has always been strength in numbers and comfort in camaraderie.

You must find allies in this battle for the heart and soul of your children. Be bold. Take the first step. Start the conversation with other parents and you just might be surprised at how many of them are actually longing for help and a return to the time when neighbors helped neighbors reinforce strong moral values for their kids. Here are just a few places to look for allies:

In a Faith Community

The first place you should look for allies is in your faith community. A large and growing body of social science research shows what a huge difference religious faith makes in our everyday lives. It's no overstatement, in fact, to say that religion makes civil society possible. Without it, just about every indicator of human misery would be off the charts.

My husband and I have raised our three children in a loving, Christian household and in a church with people who share our values. The friendships and support we have found there have done more to help us raise children of character than anything else, and the very act of attending church together also brings us closer as a family.

Pat Fagan, one of the nation's premier social-science scholars and researchers sifted through countless studies that show the remarkable effect of religious practice (including attending church) has on marriage, divorce, child-rearing, drug and alcohol abuse, out-of-wedlock births—even mental and physical health.

I was pleased to see that there are many benefits of being involved in faith community, and that they are nearly universal. Fagan reports, for instance, on how practicing faith brings parents and children closer:

> *Compared with mothers who did not consider religion important, those who deemed religion to be very important rated their relationship with their child significantly higher... When mothers and their children share the same level of religious practice, they experience better relationships with one another. For instance, when 18-year-olds attended religious services with approximately the same frequency as their mothers, the mothers reported significantly better relationships with them, even many years later... mothers who became more religious throughout the first 18 years of their child's life*

reported a better relationship with that child, regardless of the level of their religious practice before the child was born.

The same holds true for fathers:

Compared with fathers who had no religious affiliation, those who attended religious services frequently were more likely to monitor their children, praise and hug their children, and spend time with their children. In fact, fathers' frequency of religious attendance was a stronger predictor of paternal involvement in one-on-one activities with children than were employment and income—the factors most frequently cited in the academic literature on fatherhood.

How about adolescent sexual behavior? Fagan notes that traditional values and religious beliefs were among the most common factors teens cite to explain why they are abstaining from sex. In addition, the use of cigarettes and the abuse of alcohol and drugs drop significantly among those who are religiously active.

He also wrote, "In the vast majority of the studies reviewed, an increase in religious practice was associated with having greater hope and a greater sense of purpose in life."

Here are few more positive results that Dr. Fagan says are correlated with being in a community of faith:

- Churchgoers are more likely to be married, less likely to be divorced or single, and more likely to manifest high levels of satisfaction in marriage.
- Religious belief and practice contribute substantially to the formation of personal moral criteria and sound moral judgment.

- Regular religious practice generally inoculates individuals against a host of social problems, including suicide, drug abuse, out-of-wedlock births, crime, and divorce.
- The regular practice of religion also encourages such beneficial effects on mental health as a much lower risk of depression (a modern epidemic) and suicide, greater self-esteem, and greater family and marital happiness.
- In repairing damage caused by alcoholism, drug addiction, and marital breakdown, religious belief and practice are a major source of strength and recovery.

Obviously, churches aren't perfect—they are, after all, composed of imperfect people—but the results of attending church are undeniable. Solid churches are composed of people whose faith in God guides them through troubles, whose values help steer them away from cultural garbage, and who are trying to protect their children's hearts, minds, and souls. If you're looking for the best possible environment for your family in this crazy culture, head to a good church.

In Your Neighborhood

Wow, how America's concept of neighborhood has changed over the years! We live such busy lives that many of us don't even know our neighbors, much less what is important to them. If you don't know everyone on your street and on the street behind your house, take the next six months to make your way around and have a chat with every family. Identifying possible allies right-next-door can help you—and them—in countless ways. You'll also be able to figure out which houses you and your children should avoid. In addition, you can identify the needs of those right outside your door, and then create a plan with your teens on how to help. Are there elderly people down the street who need assistance with yard work? Is there a frazzled young mother who needs your counsel? Is there a single parent who could use a hand and a friend? Knowing and being involved in your neighborhood can expand the borders of your home and do you, your children, and your neighbors a world of good.

Among the parents of kids your kids already hang out with

As my children grew into teens I began to realize that I had no real information about many of the families of their new friends. Teens go to high school and suddenly have a mile-long list of friends and acquaintances. They start driving and end up visiting homes I haven't been to. It was so much easier to keep track when I had to drive them everywhere! With the convenience of having a teen that can drive herself around (and run errands for me!) comes an added level of parental responsibility. I have to work harder to gather information on the families and homes she is visiting. Kristin knows that she needs to call me from the home phone of any new friend she visits. This little trick does three things.

1) I know exactly where she is calling from and can add the number to my contact list
2) I can introduce myself to the parents and have a quick discussion about adult supervision, the activities that are going on, etc.
3) It puts the parents on notice that I care.

And, of course, I've had the discussion with Kristin about the three uncompromising reasons of when she must leave a home immediately.

1) the presence of alcohol or drugs
2) a lack of adult supervision
3) entertainment or behavior that is in conflict with what we allow in our home.

I've learned through the years that I can trust her on this, but knowing the parents provides an extra level of intelligence for me and protection for her.

I also take extra effort to get to know the teens that come into my home. Ours is a very open home filled with mobs of teenagers. Since the kids are now driving themselves over and catching rides with friends (rather than parents), I always make it a point to ask newcomers to call their parents and hand me the phone so I can say hello. You'd be surprised at how many parents are pleasantly surprised to receive such a call. Once again, I've found that some of them have quiet concerns about who their children spend time with, but for a variety of reasons, have never bothered to make the call. Placing a quick ring helps me identify which parents share my values, and assures them that I am vigilant about taking care of the minors in my home.

Through sports and other group youth activities

Whether your kids run track, play in the orchestra, or participate in other group youth activities, it's always a great idea to spend time with the parents while you attend the games, concerts, and other events. Make the effort to chat with other moms and dads, give kids rides to practices, and help out with the fund-raisers. Your child will love you for it (although they may not tell you) and you will be able to find parents who share your values. I'm amazed at how many parents are no longer involved in their kid's group activities once they reach high school. This is exactly the time you should be introducing yourself and looking for friendships and allies. You will also be able to identify (through the lack of their parent's involvement) children whose lives you can add meaning to. Your goal here should be to have a solid presence that allows you to be involved, but does not cramp your teen's growing need for independence. It can be a delicate balance, but if you don't make the effort to attend and connect with the kids and their families, you are missing a valuable opportunity to help create a community of parents that support and protect their children and uphold solid values.

FROM MY HOME TO YOURS

If you're searching for fellow-warriors to help you combat the culture and raise your children, the following tips can help you secure new friends and allies:

Be joyful: Do you remember the phrase, "Don't worry, be happy"? It's a great reminder of how hungry people are for happiness. But it can be extremely difficult to experience joy when you are in the midst of a cultural battle. People are drawn to those who are calm and filled with joy. No one wants to be around a complaining, bitter mom who is viewed as hating everything about the society around her! People seek to be with people who are positive. See it as your job to help parents, teachers, and youth group leaders to be "Happy Warriors." Encourage other parents, build their joy of parenting, and remind them that being a mom is the most wonderful blessing of all. The Bible teaches us that if we ask God for his help, and thank him for his blessings, then we will have a deep and abiding peace even in the midst of the battle. It also teaches us that the joy of God can be our strength.

Be brave: Work together with those who share your values and refuse to be afraid of those who are against you. Fear is enemy number one—fear of disapproval, snide remarks, and the evil the media throws your way can quickly kill your spirits and efforts. Think of yourself as a Conqueror. You are a voice for the innocent, a champion for what is highest and best, and a warrior for truth. Don't let anyone steal your vision of the best possible childhood and future for your child.

Secure Allies in the Battle

Be kind: While standing strong, everyone around you—especially your spouse and children—should see that you are gentle and kind. But that's hard to do—when I'm frustrated or feel attacked, or aggravated, it's very, very difficult to be gentle and kind. Our culture would teach us that it's enough to be "tolerant." But the great command is to do far more than just tolerate others—we are charged to treat others with love and kindness. That doesn't mean we give in or pretend like we approve of behavior we know is wrong. It means that we love other people enough, even in the midst of their displaying beliefs we may disagree with, to show them a kindness that just might open their hearts to what we have to say.

ACT NOW

Date _____

Today I determined I would not be silenced by fear, and that I would find allies to help me succeed in raising my kids to tower above the culture.

_____
Signature

I can find potential allies in

❏ my neighbors _____

❏ my child's friends' parents _____

❏ parents at my child's activities _____

❏ a church _____

❏ A new thing I'm going to try in order to find allies
in the battle_____

MORE HELP

CONCERNED FAMILIES (FATHERS, MOTHERS, AND YOUTH)

The unique three-tier organization has developed a simple system based on the priciple that the traditional family is a transforming power, and thus a "community family" can also be transforming. Concerned Fathers Against Crime, Concerned Mothers Alliance for Children, and Concerned Youth allow local churches to work together to bless their neighbors in targeted ways from working with law enforcement to working with local businesses. The end goal is public safety including protecting children from the negative influences of the culture. You can join forces with them or start a chapter in your area by visiting concernedfamilies.org.

Develop And Follow Your "Mother's Intuition" And "Father Knows Best" Instincts

THE CHALLENGE

As I talk to parents (especially mothers) in my own community and around the country, I have come to realize that many of us find ourselves frustrated by an ongoing conflict: we experience an intangible discernment about people and situations but don't always know how to act on it.

I think if we are honest with each other, one problem is that we fear the possibility of our instincts being incorrect and the actions we take looked upon by other parents as overreacting, overbearing, or overreaching. This fear ultimately causes many of us to remain silent—ignoring our instincts and disregarding our intuition as a reliable source of decision-making and parenting.

Society certainly does not help to convince us that our instincts are reliable. We're constantly told that we aren't smart enough or don't have the right skills to understand and raise our children. We are also accused of being "over-protective" and "close-minded" or "judgmental." Name-calling has always been an effective method for silencing people.

Another reason we often hesitate to take action is because it can lead to conflict with our children—especially our teens. If your mother's intuition gives you concern about one of your kid's friends, for instance, and you begin to delve deeper into the situation, your son or daughter may feel offended. If we already lack faith in our intuition in the first place, we tend to back away from acting on it in any way that would lead to potential parent-child conflict.

But ask yourself this question: How many times have you as a parent had your stomach suddenly filled with knots or a flash of doubt go through your mind about an issue, parent, or situation and later wished you had acted on that feeling? Likely, at least a few examples come to mind. Hindsight, of course, is always 20/20.

Listen to that voice inside you that says, "something isn't right here" and then act on it. As a parent, you are the first and last line of defense for your children. And as the saying goes, "Better safe, than sorry."

Regardless of what you may call it, undeniably women, in particular, possess a unique and mysterious kind of discernment we often refer to as "women's intuition." It may be nearly impossible to define, but I think each of us can remember a specific time when we experienced a feeling of warning or discomfort that, upon reflection, could only be described as our intuition. And ladies, when we become mothers, the ability to discern situations grows even sharper. I believe that the Lord gives parents that instinct to protect our children. It *can* be trusted, and it should not be ignored. It is something God gave you in abundance as a mother, and as mysterious as it is, it is very real. Our mother's intuition is something we need to come to trust and is an essential tool we must use to protect our children. As mothers, we also have a need to understand, and connect with, our kids unlike anybody else. We should feel confident in acting on the warnings we experience from this connection.

And fathers, there is a reason why a show like "Father Knows Best" was so popular. It's because loving dads do watch out for their families, and they do sacrifice and go the extra mile to connect to their sons and daughters. Loving dads have always weighed all the options to figure out what is best for their children. Of course, that show aired at a time when men were actually respected, and expected to take care of their families. Many of today's television commercials and sitcoms portray dads as wimpy, ignorant, and stupid. We are led to believe that they are useless and disposable. I cringe every time I see them. It would be interesting to see what effect it would have on real dads if the media started showing more programs with intact family units in which TV dads actually model what a good father looks like. It makes me wonder, is TV imitating life, or is life imitating television?

It was horribly wrong when shows of long-ago portrayed women as weak—it was downright sexist. So why is it acceptable to now turn around and do the same to men? With a barrage of media aimed at destroying masculinity, it's no wonder that it isn't "politically correct" to declare that "Father Knows Best." Perhaps that's partly why many fathers fail to exert their opinions anymore.

I remember the first time I held each of my children in my arms. I was overcome by the urge to take care of my baby and would have done anything it took to protect the precious little bundle. Most of us would take a bullet for our kids. So, we must ask ourselves, why aren't we also as willing to do something a little less heroic, and a lot less costly, like install an internet filter to protect them from child predators who might stalk them online? When polled about internet usage in their homes, the majority of parents said they have concerns about the content of what their children might be viewing. Yet, these same parents also said they had never taken any action to ensure their kids' online safety. The intuition is right, but the inaction is puzzling. What has caused you to ignore your instinct?

Proverbs 27:12 says, "The prudent see danger and take refuge, but the simple keep going and suffer for it." The warning here is clear: When we understand there is danger and take action to protect ourselves, we are wise. But when we sense harm and ignore it, we are fools and will pay the price. The bigger problem is that when you are a parent who exercises bad judgment, your children will often suffer, too.

IN YOUR SHOES

We must also help our children to develop their own intuition. My friend, Rebecca, told me how her own father took great care to develop her inner voice:

Rebecca and her dad have always been very close. She was an extremely verbal and socially mature child—sort of like a mini adult—by the age of five. You could often find her conversing with adults around her (much to their entertainment), and her father consciously treated his carefree little princess like a person of intelligence and importance. He always asked her what she thought about the people they encountered. And he invited her to do the same of him. He didn't ask what she thought about someone's haircut, of their choice of shoes, or other characteristics visible to the eye; instead, he helped her to cultivate a habit of looking deeper at people upon their first meeting and he constantly evaluated her initial intuitive reaction to them. In this way her father uniquely helped

Develop and Follow Your "Mother's Intuition"...

Rebecca develop an unprecedented relational maturity—bringing to her attention her 'women's intuition,' if you will, from a very early age. Through the years this continued, and she soon became acutely aware of a certain 'intangible yet distinct' discomfort that embodied her around certain people. Most often this first impression never fully went away even after continued interaction or exposure to the person. Note: this was something she experienced with only a handful of people and in a handful of situations. Every time she would express this 'uncomfortable' feeling to her father he would always look her steadily in the eyes and say the same thing, 'Trust that feeling, Rebecca. The Lord gives some people, and especially women, a discernment of people that should not be ignored. Whenever you sense this kind of discomfort, danger, or unease—trust it. It is very real.' And in her case it certainly turned out to be. Whether it was three different 'Christian' men with whom she had become acquainted through church who were later found to have had affairs with other men's wives; or later in life when she trusted that deep warning and avoided going to dinner with someone who later put a friend in a threatening position. Over and over again she has seen how trusting her intuition has saved her from various dangers that otherwise could not have been foreseen. I am convinced that because Rebecca's father took great care to develop her intuition, she has a honed inner compass that might have otherwise gone off kilter. Society, after all, does not trust us to listen to our consciences and the still, small voice inside of us. Instead, it often lures us to danger with empty promises of, 'Everyone's doing it, you'll be fine.' And, 'That star or politician can't be that bad, because he is so popular with masses of people.' We are often led to believe that we are odd and alone in our misgivings about others. But Rebecca's story shows us that we can help our children to develop discernment about people and situations.

FROM MY HOME TO YOURS

Remember the prayer I quoted in the Chapter 9 "Write a Letter to Your Teen"? One of the basic skills the author of that prayer, the apostle Paul, wanted for people to develop was their discernment. This is also referred to as judgment, and understanding. How do we do that? Rebecca's father showed us the truth of the biblical admonishment in Hebrews that "teaching discernment comes from constant practice to distinguish between good and evil."

Discernment can be defined as "acuteness of judgment and understanding." Intuition is described by Webster's as "a keen and quick insight." Thankfully, for all of us, discernment isn't something we have to be born with—it's something we can all develop with lots of practice. We also become more able to make those "keen and quick" insights into people and situations when we listen to, and act, on that inner feeling. But beware: the more you set your intuition aside, don't exercise your own good judgment, or ignore the difference between good and evil, the weaker your power of discernment becomes. Plainly put, you lose the ability to know the difference between good and bad. And if you or your kids have lost the sensitivity to know right from wrong, it becomes less likely that you will choose what is good, fair, and just.

When I was a child, my mother used to tell me, "If you feel the hair rising on the back of your neck, then something isn't right." It was her way of warning me to learn to be discerning, and to trust myself when I felt uncomfortable with a situation. She was right. There have been many times when I've just walked away from an "opportunity" for no other reason than that it didn't feel right. I try to teach my children to do the same. And you know what happens when you listen to your intuition? It gets better and better. When you use the insight you have, your ability to discern becomes stronger.

I heard a story on the radio recently that perfectly illustrates how easy it is to lose your way when you ignore your intuition and focus only on the pleasant. I didn't catch the name of the person sharing it, but I am eternally grateful that he did:

> *A pastor was relating how he went to Hawaii and had the opportunity to go snorkeling. There, in crystal clear waters, he could put his head just under the surface and see amazingly beautiful, colorful fish all around him. He waded out about waist deep, and was mesmerized by the beauty. The guide told him that he would be able to get a far better view if he got on a raft and floated while he watched. The pastor complied, even though he knew the water was getting deep, and lay down on the raft in such a way that he could stick his face just below the surface and slightly lift it every now and then for a breath. He saw so many lovely creatures, and got so caught up in the glory of it all that he no longer paid attention to where he was. After some time, he heard a noise and looked up to see a rescue boat pulling toward him. Startled, he turned around and looked toward the shore—which was so far away he could no longer see the people on the beach! He had ignored his initial warning system, and focused instead on the fun he was having—he had become so mesmerized by the dazzling colors that he had drifted into grave danger before he knew it. This is exactly what can happen to us and our children if we ignore our intuition—if we lose sight of the truth and become blinded by the dazzle.*

ACT NOW

Date _____

Today I vowed to never doubt my own conscience and intuition. I started to trust my ability to discern, and pledged to practice following it.

_____

Signature

Install Parental Controls On Your Televisions— And Be The Ultimate Control

THE CHALLENGE

According to the American Academy of Pediatrics, the average child views television for approximately four hours a day. This astounding fact should be enough to give every parent cause for alarm.

Aside from the fact that every hour spent watching television is usually an hour wasted, it is also an hour that takes the place of doing something good or healthy—like reading, exercising, interacting with family and peers, and enjoying the outdoors. To make matters worse, many of those wasted hours are saturated with violence, sexual activity, drug use, crafty advertisements, and other pernicious media material that your child—and probably you in many cases—should simply not be watching.

An article by *Time-Scout Monitor* writes that, "Television has become so entrenched in family life that it needs to be considered a socializing agent comparable to parents and educators. 98 percent of the 75 million households in the United States own a television set, and these sets are turned on an average of 7 hours a day."

The standards for what is permissible in primetime are at an all-time low on both broadcast and cable stations. Steaming sex-laden shows geared toward young people are now airing at the peak of the viewing hour, accessible to children of any age. To make matters worse, most digital or satellite television contracts come with scores of channels airing pornography and countless variations of MTV, VH1, and the like. Without limitations, TV is simply not safe for anyone—especially those with developing minds.

And, of course, as every parent knows by now, it's not just the programming you have to worry about—it's often the commercials, too. How many of us have frantically tried to grab the remote control in the middle of an ad on erectile dysfunction? How many pre-teen and teen girls have been embarrassed when an ad on feminine hygiene comes on while boys are in the room? And how many of us are sick and tired of adult males being portrayed in commercials as lazy, ignorant, and stupid?

The fact is, in today's television world, you can never be certain that your family is safe from values that run counter to yours or that your kids are protected from information far above their level of maturity to understand.

The psychological damage done to children and teens by exposure to harmful television has been proven and documented by countless scientific and social studies. Research also shows how television programming can affect behavior.

A 2008 study by the RAND Corporation reveals what many parents have known in our guts for a long time: kids who watch sex on television are more likely to engage in sexual activity. The study followed the viewing habits of teenagers over a four-year period and found, specifically, that teens who watch high levels of sexual activity are also twice as likely to be involved in a pregnancy as kids who have limited exposure. The report also revealed that such consumers are also more likely to engage in sex at younger ages than their peers.

The University of Michigan's Health System, as compiled by Kyla Boyse, R.N., lists the following dangers to your child from overexposure to television:

■ TV viewing is probably replacing activities in your child's life that you would rather they do (things like playing with friends, being physically active, getting fresh air, reading, playing imaginatively, doing homework, and doing chores).

■ Kids who spend more time watching TV (both with and without parent and siblings present) spend less time interacting with family members.

■ Excessive TV viewing can contribute to poor grades, sleep problems, behavior problems, obesity, and risky behavior.

■ Most children's programming does not teach what parents say they want their children to learn; many shows are filled with stereotypes, violent solutions to problems, and mean or disrespectful behavior.

■ Advertisers target kids, and on average, children see tens of thousands of TV commercials each year, including some 2,000 beer and wine ads.

The University also lists on its website the following dangers to exposure to violence on TV, pulled from various child health studies:

■ An average American child will see 200,000 violent acts and 16,000 murders on TV by age 18.

- Two-thirds of all programming contains violence.
- Programs designed for children more often contain violence than adult TV.
- Most violent acts go unpunished on TV and are often accompanied by humor. The consequences of human suffering and loss are rarely depicted.
- Many shows glamorize violence. TV often promotes violent acts as a fun and effective way to get what you want, without consequences.
- Even in G-rated, animated movies and DVDs, violence is common—often as a way for the good characters to solve their problems. Every single U.S. animated feature film produced between 1937 and 1999 contained violence, and the amount of violence with intent to injure has increased over the years.
- Children imitate the violence they see on TV. Children under age eight cannot tell the difference between reality and fantasy, making them more vulnerable to learning from and adopting as reality the violence they see on TV.
- Repeated exposure to TV violence makes children less sensitive toward its effects on victims and the human suffering it causes. Viewing TV violence reduces inhibitions and leads to more aggressive behavior.
- Watching television violence can have long-term effects:
  - A 15-year-long study by University of Michigan researchers found that the link between childhood TV-violence viewing and aggressive and violent behavior persists into adulthood.
  - A 17-year-long study found that teenaged boys who grew up watching more TV each day are more likely to commit acts of violence than those who watched less.

Install Parental Controls on Your Televisions...

The only real solution to the many problems listed above is to take control of the television viewing habits in your home. Some parents may choose to eliminate all television, but I don't recommend this. The TV is not the problem—the problem is lack of parental oversight. There are so many wonderful, educational, and inspirational programs on television that it would be very sad to block it all. There's also the risk of unintentionally glamorizing it as a taboo that your child may try to break in other places. Regardless of your tactic, you must take control. Fortunately, with the parental controls available today, it's easier than ever to screen out much of the harmful or objectionable material. It may take an hour or so to set up the controls and understand how they work, but my goodness, one hour of your time can keep your child from watching thousands of hours of raunchy programming over many years. Just do it. And remember, you can't rely solely on the ratings system or the judgment of others—you have to set limits, hours, and be available to help your kids sort through garbage on your own terms. The first step is to install a blocking technology or use a tool such as TIVO to record worthwhile programming sans commercials. The second step is to vow to be the ultimate control. You just can't fully depend on any device to make personal judgments for you based on your children and your values—and you can't depend on the technology to always work.

You've got to remember that your kids are much more technologically savvy than you will ever be. As one young man informed me while I was writing this book, "Kids can be pretty ingenious about breaking codes and you will never know it—especially high schoolers." Of course, that statement got me to delve much deeper into what he was getting at. With some reluctance, but with also a level of maturity in understanding that parents need to know how easy codes are to break, he proceeded to tell me that it took him and his brother about an hour-and-a-half to figure out a way to discover the password on the parental controls. "We put little marks of highlighter on each of the numbers on the controller. We told Dad that we wanted to watch something from the movies-on-demand section, and we gave him the remote control to punch in the password. After he ordered the movie and left the room, we turned on a black light to see what numbers were smudged and then we wrote out each possible combination. We punched them all in until we figured it out—the passcode was 3906."

So what are the lessons learned here? A few things: 1) Change your passcode—often. 2) Your kids want to prove that they are more techno advanced than you are—and they will do it just to show that they are. 3) No matter how good your kids are, the media is always there tempting them. 4) Life is full of surprises! There's a lot going on that you don't know about!

IN YOUR SHOES

When Gwen was six, her mother left her in front of the television watching Sesame Street while she made dinner. While Mom was in the kitchen cooking, Gwen picked up the remote. She was at an observant age, and had recently watched her father casually flipping channels and found it interesting. She flipped through some sports games, news, and family dramas. She couldn't quite figure out how to get back to Sesame Street so she kept pressing the button.

Some channels later, she landed on a scene with a nude woman showering, and eerie music playing in the background. A man with a large knife was slinking towards her in the dark. She was terrified.

Gwen had stumbled onto the infamous shower scene in the horror movie Psycho, in which a naked, showering woman is brutally stabbed to death. Transfixed in horror, she watched the entire scene.

Install Parental Controls on Your Televisions...

Her mother returned to find her blanched and unable to speak. By that time, the commercials had come on, so her mother did not know what she had watched, but she knew Gwen had seen something she should not have.

That night, Gwen sobbed for hours and was unable to sleep. For months, she had trouble sleeping and ridding herself of the horrible images she had seen. Her mother frequently awoke to hear her crying and often had to lie in bed with her for hours to soothe her.

It wasn't until twenty years later that Gwen shared the scene that had haunted her throughout her childhood! Her story is a sad reminder that children cannot easily erase the images that are put into their minds. Television marks us like permanent ink. Whether it's gory violence, graphic sexual innuendo, or some other garbage, once we have viewed it, it's there to stay. We may not remember it as often as Gwen, but it undoubtedly affects us in some negative way.

A man named Poppy shared the positive results that discussing, monitoring, and explaining viewing rules have had on his children with me via e-mail:

"We have four boys and they are very active and interested in movies, cartoons, and video games like most kids. However, I have trained them that there are certain shows and games that they won't be seeing, and I always explain why. So it thrills me now when something questionable will come on TV (they DO NOT, and NEVER WILL have a TV in their rooms) and they will turn around and look at me, because they already know when something is not right. I have also overheard them telling their friends, "We're not allowed to watch that." I feel that when you explain the reasoning

behind the rule, children begin to make informed and wise choices at an early age. Our boys regularly go to the movies and watch age-appropriate programming, so there is no sense of deprivation. They do participate in the culture—but with wisdom and guidance based on our worldview."

FROM MY HOME TO YOURS

In addition to using parental controls, the American Academy of Pediatrics suggests practical ways that you can take control of your family television set:

- ❏ **Set reasonable limits.** Limit your children's use of TV, movies, and video and computer games. Do not let your children watch TV while doing homework. Do not put a TV in your children's bedrooms.
- ❏ **Plan what to watch.** Instead of flipping through channels, use a program guide and the TV ratings to help you and your children choose which shows to watch. Turn the TV on to watch the program and turn it off when it is over.
- ❏ **Watch TV with your children.** Whenever possible, watch TV with your children and talk about what they see.
- ❏ **Find the right message.** Some TV programs show people as stereotypes. If you see this, talk with your children about the real-life roles of women, the elderly, and people of other races.
- ❏ **Help your children resist commercials.** When your children ask for things they see on TV, explain that the purpose of commercials is to make people want things they may not need.

Install Parental Controls on Your Televisions...

❏ **Find something else to do.** Watching TV can become a habit for your children. Help them find other things to do like playing; reading; learning a hobby, a sport, an instrument, or an art; or spending time with family, friends, or neighbors.

❏ **Set a good example.** As a role model, limiting your own TV viewing and choosing programs carefully will help your children do the same.

❏ **Express your views.** When you like or do not like something you see on TV, make yourself heard. Stations, networks, and sponsors pay attention to letters from the public. If you think a commercial is misleading or inappropriately targeting children, write down the product name, channel, and time you saw the commercial and describe your concerns.

ACT NOW

Date _____

   Today I learned how to use the V-Chip (See "More Help") or the parental controls on my remote control. I also vowed to be the one to determine how much, when, and what my children watch on television.

_____
Signature

MORE HELP

- Unless you bought your television in the dark ages, it contains something called a "V-Chip," which allows you to filter TV programs by rating. If you are unsure of how to use this great tool, visit thetvboss.com for a tutorial on how to program it. You can block individual channels and shows and lock them with a password. There are also several tamper-proof "TV time management" devices on the market that allow parents to set limits on how much time is spent watching TV. You can even buy a special remote for children (a "Weemote") with large, simple buttons that can be programmed to access only approved TV channels.

- The website of the National Cable & Telecommunications Association is filled with great advice on other parental controls. NOTE: Your local NCTA affiliate (there's probably one in your town) will provide free parental controls to customers who request them. Just log on to controlyourtv.org to learn more. You can also sign-up to receive free e-mail updates on how to establish good viewing habits in your home. I have the controls on my digital-cable access, and I love being able to block programming based on rating, channel, or other criteria.

Be Your Family's Movie Critic

THE CHALLENGE

There's nothing like a cold, rainy or winter day to make you think about taking the family to the local multiplex and seeing a movie. Grab some popcorn, forget your worries for a couple hours, and enter that larger-than-life world of imagination and spectacle, of heroes and villains.

Warning: Your choices are going to be somewhat limited if your aim is wholesome family entertainment. What's showing at the movies this week? Hmm, the story about how the world's most infamous cannibal acquired his taste for his fellow man? An apocalyptic future world in which the human race is threatened with extinction?

How about spending the evening with a deranged killer that stalks young people?

Why on earth do parents actually pay for their children to explore the depths of human depravity? Simply put, most parents just aren't paying attention.

And what about the video store? Next time you go, count how many titles you see that feature raw sex, violence, or disloyalty—the list goes on. Take a few minutes to watch how many kids check out movies filled with messages that undermine the strong character traits most parents want their children to develop. It's crazy to hope that our kids will grow up understanding the importance of fidelity, purity, and honesty when they are digesting a steady diet of garbage—all usually paid for by mom and dad.

As the Dove Foundation, an excellent online family media rating system, notes on its website dove.org:

"For years we have watched the morals and attitudes of the entertainment industry slowly creep into our society."

However, just because Hollywood's standards are sliding, does not mean we as parents must follow suit. It is up to us to determine what we will allow into our home and how we will equip our children to make the right moral choices at the movies.

In his article "Marquee Madness," written for The Heritage Foundation, president Dr. Edwin Feulner wrote about the then-recently released Federal Trade Commission report documenting the damaging effect of American pop culture on children. Many were concerned the report's findings might lead to calls for greater censorship. Dr. Feulner wrote:

"If parents want to protect their kids *and* avoid censorship, they must be the ones pressuring Hollywood to change. It's the only way to guarantee a happy ending to what has so far been a sad, sad story."

If we want to live in an ownership society that emphasizes personal responsibility, we as parents cannot waste time wagging fingers at Hollywood. Parents must take responsibility for their own children. Hollywood will follow their cues. They want to make profitable films! PG-13 and R-rated films don't make the most money—not by a long shot. Ironically, it's G- and PG-rated films that prove to be the most lucrative. Dove examined the average profits per film between 1989 and 2003, and it found that G-rated films produced *11 times* more profit than R-rated films. If parents continue to vamp up the demand for wholesome movies, Hollywood will produce them. There is hope. Dove has partnered with Twentieth Century Fox to promote family entertainment by placing a Dove "seal of approval" on wholesome films. Left to their own devices, Hollywood moguls will continue to turn the stories of childhood heroes into disturbingly dark films

A recent Batman movie, *The Dark Knight*, provides a perfect case-in-point. The film broke every box office record in history. It also heavily targeted youth. It was, after all, a film about a comic book hero! Yet there was wide ranging agreement amongst critics that the film, rated PG-13, should have been rated R, and was definitely not kid-friendly. Christopher Orr of *The New Republic* wrote, "This is *not* a film for children, and the MPAA should be ashamed of its PG-13 acquiescence."

What did the movie actually contain? "Violent shooting, people being run over by a bus, a gas device placed in a man's throat, a man being impaled by a pencil, a man's face burned in half revealing burnt flesh, eye socket and bone, an explosive placed in a man's stomach, sexual innuendo, countless curse words and scenes of brutal and bloody violence," just to list a few. It got off the hook though, because there were no F-words.

One twenty-four-year-old man wrote to me that it was by far "the most hauntingly, disturbing PG-13" he had ever seen and would "recommend exercising great discretion before seeing the film, even as an adult." Yet the movie industry would like you to think it's perfectly appropriate for your thirteen-year-old son or daughter, and the movie makers intended for kids of all ages to come and see it.

Something is wrong with this picture.

The fact is, you can't rely on the Hollywood rating system to make wise viewing choices for your family. To begin with, there has been a steady decline in the ratings system with industry standards becoming more lax as the years go by. A movie that would have received a PG-rating ten years ago, for instance, could easily be a G-rated movie today.

On the flip-side, some movies that receive an R-rating might actually contain stories of violence and war that are a critical part of a larger story with a positive message. Two examples of R-rated movies that might be appropriate and actually beneficial in teaching values to teens come to mind: *The Passion of the Christ*, the story of the crucifixion of Jesus and *The Patriot*, a historical-fiction movie that underscores the valiant vision and sacrifices in the struggle for America's freedom.

The point is that you as the parent need to be the movie-critic for your children. What might be inappropriate for your eleven-year-old might be incredibly valuable in helping to underscore lessons of morality for your sixteen-year-old. Don't let other adults make the final decisions for you! The easiest way to make selections is to start with a trusted source for movie reviews, and then go from there in making your decisions. Several great resources are listed in the More Help section.

IN YOUR SHOES

I wonder how many conversations about movies between parents and children have ended in tears. Children, and especially teenagers, see movies as an opportunity to exercise freedom and choice, along with the right to engage with today's culture and their friends. In a time when the social community in America is in serious decline, the theatre has become one of the most popular places for children to "hang out."

But gore and promiscuity seem to have become the keystone and bedrock of most flicks being produced these days. The key is to find an age-appropriate system that allows your children to have a say while allowing you to take responsible steps to protect your sons and daughters from the whims of crazy movie-makers who despise your world-view.

Alice, a young adult, recently shared with me how movies were the greatest strain on her relationship with her mother as a teen, and what her family did to tackle the problem and teach her to use discretion.

Alice was independent, responsible, and took pride in making good choices; she also loved films. Her mother was also strong-willed, and took pride in making sure that Hollywood trash stayed far away from her daughter.

When Friday nights rolled around, Alice loved heading to the theatre with friends or to the store to pick out something lively and engaging. But she dreaded the pending conversation with mom, and mom dreaded the argument, and tears, that almost always ensued. Most of the arguments centered on whether or not Alice should be allowed to watch R-rated movies.

One night, the argument over a weekend flick went too far. Both mom and daughter wound up in tears, and Alice's father had had enough.

They all sat down for a brainstorming session, and after several hours, decided on a "movie contract." Alice, who was then 16, was given full discretion over PG-13 movies. There was one caveat: For every PG-13 movie she chose, she was required to write a brief summary about why she chose it, why it was rated PG-13, and whether or not it was a worthwhile movie.

When it came to R-rated movies, Alice could select three R movies a year, all of which had to have some grounding in historical accuracy. The same reporting requirement stood.

If her parents felt as though she was making thoughtful and responsible choices according to their family movie guide, Alice's movie selection rights would be re-evaluated and expanded after the course of one year. If she failed to produce a report, or continually made unwise choices, her movie-choosing rights would be constricted.

They never had another argument over movies again. Now that is a happy ending.

Alice's parents basically gave her ownership rights over part of her decisions about films. They shifted a significant portion of the responsibility of making ethical choices to her, with some guidance. They familiarized her with their movie guide and its objective standards, which allowed her to better judge how to make a good decision about a PG-13 or R movie. They made it clear that her choices would be measured in large part against their criteria for a wholesome film. They established a clear and consistent policy that took into account their daughter's level of maturity, their parental responsibility to impart their values to her, and the right to make the final decisions. Best of all, they were able to come up with a solution they were all happy with.

Be Your Family's Movie Critic

Date _____

    Today I deliberately began to establish a movie-rating system for my children based on our values, and their ages and maturity.

_____

Signature

MORE HELP

Take heart, parents: There are great films made by great artists featuring great stories that your family will enjoy. Lots of them. But you owe it to your children and their developing character to do your homework in finding them.

- One of my favorite sites is pluggedinonline.org. I used it many times when my daughter or sons called from a friend's house to ask for permission to watch a movie. When it is necessary to give a "yes" or "no" answer very quickly, I go to the site, type in the name of the movie in question, and Presto! have a thorough review pop up on the screen. The site has also enabled me to make alternative suggestions if my gut tells me the particular requested movie isn't right for us.

- Dove.org, run by The Dove Foundation, promotes family-friendly entertainment in a refreshingly positive way. It also encourages the creation of good movies by reviewing films for parents and by putting its "Family-Approved" seal on those that actually provide clean entertainment. And their message gets through. According to Ralph Winter, producer of the "X-Men" films, among other titles, "The Dove Foundation provides a valuable service for those of us working in Hollywood trying to reach values-based audiences." If you count yourself among that audience, you owe it to yourself and your children to speak up in support of good films—and vote with your wallet. That's the best way to ensure a happy ending.

- Movieguide.org and the magazine by the same name are dedicated "to redeeming the values of the mass media according to biblical principles by influencing media executives to adopt higher standards imbued with Christian and traditional family values, and by informing and equipping moral people in America and around the world, especially parents,

continued

Be Your Family's Movie Critic

MORE HELP

families and Christians, to make wise media choices based on the biblical worldview." Many reviews are available for no charge on the website, and a subscription to the site or the magazine will provide you with more in-depth information.

■ Familyentertainmentcentral.org is also an excellent source for reviewing your family's entertainment. It is a veritable one-stop shopping mall for all the reviews and articles you need to make anxiety-free media choices for your children.

Tell Your Children What Makes A True Hero, And Pledge To Be A Hero, Too

THE CHALLENGE

Have you seen any true heroes lately?

By definition, a hero is someone who has done something noble and good, something worthy of our admiration and respect. Right?

Nowadays, the answer to that question is not so clear. Today's generation is redefining heroism, and not for the better. And who can blame them? The pickings are slim when choosing a hero from modern culture, be it pop or political, athletic or artistic.

It seems like every day that we hear about a once upstanding politician mired in a sex scandal or a Hall of Fame athlete caught doping. Even comic book superheroes are turned into haunting and violent characters for the big screen in films like *The Dark Knight* or *Iron-man*.

Janet, a young woman teaching in the New York public school system, learned just how low the hero-bar has fallen for today's children when she did an exercise on role models with her fourth grade social studies class, which she shared with me over e-mail.

She assigned as homework a small project where each child had to think about someone they considered to be their role model, someone they aspired to be like when they grew up. They then had to draw a picture and give a presentation to the class.

Janet was curious to see who her children looked up to. The next day, the class tumbled in with their drawings. As the presentations began, Janet was horrified.

Students chose figures such as Madonna, 50 Cent, and James Bond. One student just wrote that he just wanted to be a "hitman" when he grew up.

More than half of the boys' drawings included violent imagery such as guns or blood. And most of the girls drew a woman who was in some way a pop icon, a majority of the time dressed in something skimpy.

If these are the figures our children seek to emulate, then we are in serious trouble.

As the primary adults in our kids' lives, we can begin to teach our children about the true meaning of heroism by modeling virtue in the home. We must aspire to be role models to our children and to teach them where to look for true heroism.

And if you are a single parent or a grandparent blessed with raising a child or teen, don't ever let society tell you that you can't be a hero too.

IN YOUR SHOES

We cannot afford to let our children grow up worshipping Playboy bunnies and explicit rap artists. As U.S. Supreme Court Justice Clarence Thomas remarked in a speech about his wonderful book, My Grandfather's Son, "A free society will not survive without people of character who foster virtue through example. Doing good deeds and hard work is habit forming and ultimately builds character." Indeed. Justice Thomas' entire book is a testament and tribute to the power of his personal hero—his grandfather. Abandoned by his own father at a very young age, the Justice describes how even a poor, black, fatherless child in the segregated South rose above his circumstances because there was a powerful force for good that guided him. Justice Thomas speaks eloquently and respectfully of the man who rescued him from the life of waste that so often claimed the souls of young black males in the 1950s. His grandfather was the steely, emotionally distant "Daddy"—a man who wouldn't take "no" for an answer (from his grandson or society) and who taught the young Thomas how hard work, character, and loyalty could overcome even the worst of circumstances. Thomas recalls one of his grandfather's favorite sayings: "Old Man Can't is dead—I helped bury him."

Teaching children about the role models within our own families is a great way to talk about heroism. It can help your child connect to noble behavior in a personal way, and see that everyday, imperfect people can do things worthy of great esteem. My life has been filled with heroes. My own father was a giant of a man who understood that fathers and mothers are the most important forces in their children's lives. And when I married my knight-in-shining armor over 20 years ago, God blessed me with another hero: my father-in-law.

Papa John quickly became an important part of my life. As I grew to know and love him and my mother-in-law over the years, it was quite evident why my husband is a man of strong character and selfless love.

What follows is an excerpt from a column I wrote about my father-in-law. I share it again as a reminder that we often forget that real heroes can be found within our own families.

A couple of years ago, my husband and I took his parents and our kids to the Fantasy of Flight Museum, a private collection in Polk City, Florida, boasting what may be the world's largest assemblage of airworthy vintage aircraft. Andy and I felt the trip would bring a better understanding of what Papa John, a World War II vet, and the Greatest Generation went through to protect America's freedom some years ago.

Papa John wore his best poker face as he climbed carefully through the bomb-bay doors and into the fuselage, his grandsons scrambling in close behind. But it had to have been an emotional moment for him. During World War II, he served with the 450th bomb group, as a nose gunner in a B-24 Liberator, making runs from Italy into southern Europe. Unlike many, he returned to wed, raise a family, and see his kids raise families of their own.

Even with its bomb racks empty, the bomb bay was surprisingly cramped. Between the racks, the only way forward to the flight deck and to Papa John's former battle station was a narrow girder, not even wide enough to be called a catwalk.

Negotiating that, then hunching down, and finally crawling forward, Papa John advanced as far toward the nose turret as his now-creaky knees would let him, just far enough to brush aside a patch of spider webs and peer inside through its double hatch.

He had certainly had a good view from that position, as far forward as one could possibly be in an airplane, with only a bubble of a Plexiglas between him and the frigid, onrushing air. How had he folded himself, his parachute, and other gear into that tiny space? How could he stay in that position for up to eight hours? How did it feel to be shot at the first time? What did it feel like to climb back in for a second mission? A third? And what did you do to expel the thought that the next mission might be your last?

True to form, Papa John was a fount of knowledge about all things technical. He pointed out the dials and knobs and handles, explained their purpose and how they worked. Those things seemed to come back pretty easily. But how it all felt was more difficult to put into words, maybe even to remember.

As with most of those who made it back, there has rarely been an appropriate moment to share details of those days. Even if the moment presented itself, the story is not an easy one to tell. How does one present the full context of the experience? Wanting above all to be accurate, how does one weave a complete and coherent story out of a collection of memories, some vivid and some vague, particularly when you never knew the whole story anyway? And how do you tell your story knowing that it is only a very small part of a very large undertaking? So, more often than not, their stories go untold.

The silence is part of what makes Papa John—and so many like him in the Greatest Generation—so great. It is our duty, not theirs, to collect and preserve their story. That is why it's good to build museums, write books, produce documentary films, and tell our children. It's right to recognize their sacrifice. That is the reason we establish memorial days and create memorial monuments in Washington and in hometowns across America. And it's right to thank them by stepping forward to take up the banner of service they carried so faithfully, and by working to restore an America of virtue and strong moral values.

They are the heroes about whom we must begin to teach our children.

FROM MY HOME TO YOURS

Mom and Dad, you can be the most effective hero for your kids. Despite what the educators, social scientists, or the culture tell you, the truth is that you are the primary force in your child's life. You can inspire them, teach them, care for them on a daily basis and protect them from heartache and danger countless times. Sometimes, you will see the result of your heroism and hard work in small bits and pieces. But, mostly, you can take comfort in the fact that although your son might not recognize you as his role-model right now, or that your daughter may not tell you how much she appreciates your endless sacrifices, you are having a tremendous influence. It's true that the hand that rocks the cradle rules the world. And that's also true of the hand that turns off the television when degrading material is on, that takes the car keys away from a son who has been disrespectful, or of the arms that wrap around the teenage daughter when she has experienced hurt or disappointment.

My gut has always told me that my children need my husband and me to be an active part of their daily lives. Thank the Lord we listened to our quiet instincts over the myriad other boisterous voices whose constant mantra tells parents that we are irrelevant, replaceable, and even harmful. With two sons in college and a daughter well on her way to adulthood, I've come to realize all too soon that the opportunity I have to mold and shape the hearts and lives entrusted to my care is the greatest privilege and challenge of my life. It's a challenge worthy of a hero. Yours is, too.

ACT NOW

Date _____

    Today I told my children about one of my life heroes. I discussed with them what makes true heroism, and vowed I would always strive to be a hero for them.

_____
Signature

MORE HELP

■ One excellent way to teach your child about heroes is by simply picking up a good biography. Try reading a biography of a great historical or
contemporary figure together as a family. A good one to start with is
John Keegan's short but excellent piece on Winston Churchill or David
McCullough's book on John Adams. Hillsdale College has the most ex-
pansive collection on Churchill ever written—his official biography—
which is composed of numerous volumes. It's a fabulous collection to
start adding to your personal library. Hillsdale also offers one of the
largest collections of speeches from modern leaders who are heroes in
their own right from many different fields. The speeches are published
in a monthly newsletter, *Imprimis*, to which you can subscribe, free of
charge, at Hillsdale.edu. If your child is a sports enthusiast, find books
about players and coaches that are known for their skill *and* character.
Stories about great people present a wonderful opportunity to teach
your child about the material and makeup of heroes.

■ Vision Forum has made it their job to provide both historic and contemporary books, tapes, DVD's, and even conferences and seminars
about real-life heroes who model character, sacrifice, and courage. Their
website is absolutely full of inspiring materials that can change your life
and the lives of your kids. What's particularly valuable about their products is that they encourage and equip moms and dads to be the ultimate heroes in their children's lives. Regardless of your past or
circumstances, the materials at Vision Forum will inspire you to rise up
and become the moms and dads of your child's dreams. You can access their extensive catalogue and offerings at VisionForum.org.

Teach Your Children Every Day That They Have God-Given Value

THE CHALLENGE

In today's highly competitive and busy world, kids can easily believe that their value comes from what they do versus who they are. Well-meaning moms and dads hustle and bustle their kids around from countless sports, clubs, social activities, and shopping, then back home for homework, quick dinners, and weary evenings. We wake up the next morning and start the day with stress and mayhem....only to do the whole thing all over again. In the busyness and good things we do in life, we often overlook that what our child craves is a sense of personal meaning—some signal that he is loved and valued just as he is.

The world often confuses "self-esteem" with "worth." We know today's teens struggle with doubt and feelings of inadequacy, so we create special programs and school events that gloss over the problem with "feel good" language. Our local high school recently had a day-long program they called "ROCS"—an acronym for, "Respect Others, Community, and Self." While such a program may sound wonderful and be filled with good intentions, it teaches exactly the *wrong* message: that our value comes from *how we view ourselves*. It is a man-made message that is contrary to reality. Of course we should view ourselves as having value, but the essence of our true value can't be found in our own high opinion of "self," which is a subjective standard that's vulnerable to shifting feelings. It is impossible to teach the true worth of human beings absent teaching them about God, who does not change.

Of course, the public schools are now forbidden to teach about the One that can truly provide our children with a sense of their ultimate value. This wasn't always the case. Many public schools in this country were originally started in order to teach children how to read the Bible. Prayer was a daily activity, and God was acknowledged as the source of wisdom, love, and the ability to live harmoniously with others.

Our schools today and the modern pop culture's message are void of any recognition of the intrinsic value of the individual. Our kids are taught that they are here only as a result of evolution—that they have the same worth as ancient apes; that they are simply a by-product of an accidental "Big Bang"; or that they are just some advanced form of primordial ooze that appeared billions of years ago. But, by golly, they should feel really, really good about themselves anyway!

They are also taught that a human life is of value only when it is wanted, and disposable when it is inconvenient. The mantra of "abortion on demand at anytime, for any reason" has led to the devaluation of children and humanity in general. If a baby can be killed at will by her own mother just because she has yet to take a first breath of air, how on earth can she be of any real value after she is born? We live in a world where the elderly, the sick, and the disabled are often shoved off to nursing homes away from people who can actually "contribute" to society. Many of them are left to die in loneliness, or worse yet, feel as if they have been asked to die by virtue of the fact that they have been abandoned. We even, in a growing number of cases, actively "euthanize" them.

Add to this stark reality the onslaught of media messages that teach our kids they are nothing more than animals in heat, that relationships are as disposable as tattered clothes, and that "love" is based on temporary cravings and emotions, and it's no wonder we have a generation of kids who don't know they are precious individuals with a sacred calling.

Such empty messages and vain imaginings have wreaked horrible consequences on the lives of our sons and daughters. Consider these sad facts:

- According to numerous studies, the United States has the highest teen pregnancy rate in the entire industrialized world. One out of three teens will become pregnant out-of-wedlock at least once before they are 18 years old.
- According to the Centers for Disease Control, a full fifty percent of the new cases of Sexually Transmitted Diseases reported every year is in teenagers ages 14–18.
- The Chronicles of Higher Education, which monitors trends on college campuses, reports that today's college students have the highest suicide rate of any generation before them.
- The Chronicles also report that higher and higher numbers of incoming freshman have been diagnosed with clinical depression.

■ "Cutting"—the act of taking a razor or some other sharp object and slicing your arms or legs—has become a tragic trend among teenage girls. When one middle-class teen girl was asked why she cuts herself she said, "I do it when I'm sad or lonely. It makes me feel alive." Columnist Michelle Malkin reported that one school counselor said, "70 percent of the kids here cut or know someone who does. It's cool, a trend, and acceptable."

Marian, a public school teacher in Maryland, observes:

> *Parents and politicians would do well to spend a noon hour in the cafeteria of a public school. Kids in super-tight or droopy jeans and t-shirts reading "Yes—but not with you" or "You forgot to ask if I care" shuffle through food lines. But bad fashion and rude comments are not their only common denominators. Their more defining trait is the forlorn look they share."*

The fact is every person is made in the image of God. Every child is fashioned by a loving Creator who knows and calls him by name. What a powerful message to share with our children! If God made you and knows you, then you had value before you were even born—that's before you brought home one good grade, or scored a goal for the team, or before you did your first good deed.

The value of human life is most beautifully stated in Psalm 139: 13–15:

> "For you created my inmost being; you knit me together in my mother's womb. I praise you because I am fearfully and wonderfully made; your works are wonderful, I know that full well. My frame was not hidden from you when I was made in the secret place."

I believe, as pastor Steve King of Cherrydale Baptist in Arlington, Virginia says, *"Every human life has infinite value and limitless potential."* Our children need to know this—regardless of their IQ, physical abilities, successes, failures, popularity, or emotional state at any given time.

Teaching your children they have value in God's eyes is the single greatest thing you can do for your kids. Let them know that there is a God that loves them, that knows and calls them by name. He knows how many hairs are on their head, how many concerns they have in their hearts, and what issues they struggle over.

If a child knows he has intrinsic value, just because he exists, then he begins to understand that his life has meaning and purpose. Our children must know that they are important just as they are. Kids who know they are of value are less likely to do drugs, less likely to sleep around, and able to gather a sense of purpose and mission for their futures.

And you know what else happens? They begin to love, value, and help others—just for who *they* are too. A deep sense and understanding of the love of God is something you just can't help spreading to others. Your view of your community changes. You understand that other people are of value—not because you happen to respect them—but because God has decided it is so. Such an understanding by our children could change their generation overnight.

There is a very simple five-step process that you can begin to go through today that will absolutely teach your children of their value and worth. Practicing what is known as a "blessing," dating way back from Abraham's day, will instill in your children a sense of well-being, purpose, and abiding love, and will also strengthen your relationship with them in the process.

The church I attend has what our pastor calls a "dedication" ceremony for parents of new babies. But it is also applicable and highly powerful for children of all ages. Every time I sit through the brief charge, I am reminded that my teen daughter and young adult sons need for me, as their mom, to "bless" them on a daily basis. Here are very basic—but very powerful—actions you can perform every day that will change your child's life:

- Bless your child with loving, meaningful physical touch.
- Bless your child with positive spoken words to and about them.
- Bless your child by expressing that he is a person of high value.
- Bless your child by painting a vision of a bright future for her.
- Bless your child by making an active, permanent commitment to him as a person.

IN YOUR SHOES

I asked my Townhall.com readers to share how they teach their children that they have intrinsic value in God's eyes. Among the very thoughtful and simple tips that came in are these two:

Jim said, "We go to church. I also talk about the heart—a lot. I am always saying, 'I always love you,' 'You are always important,' 'You are always special.' That, taken with the church community, makes the jump to God a very small step.

Mary offered this advice, "To help my children know that they (and others) have value in God's eyes—I listen to them, reflective listening in which I try to articulate what they're telling me. I also take my children to parish visitations so they understand that people are rich and poor, young and old, wise and foolish—and sometimes the wise ones are the ones you *least expect to be. Most of all, I turn down any activities for myself that I don't see as vital, especially if they're at night. I have seen that, if I can talk to my children before I put them to bed, they see themselves as important to me."*

Several readers suggested the importance of teaching our children to pray. A reader named Gary shared this beautiful story about how the heart of even the smallest child responds to the news that God values them and desires to communicate with them. In the process of sharing the story, Gary also offers a creative idea for how to further connect our children to God through prayer:

Our youth group gave us all a gift; a "Prayer Jar" as a thanks for helping them with a project. Not knowing exactly what a Prayer Jar was for, I got the inspiration to instruct our grandchildren that the Prayer Jar was for whispering our prayers to God.

The next day, we passed the Prayer Jar around the breakfast table and everyone thanked God for his many blessings. My grandchildren were really excited about saying prayers into the jar and continued to add prayers to it the entire day.

That night we offered up our prayers to Jesus. By whispering them into the Prayer Jar [that morning], we not only prayed then, but now we released them to Him all over again. So, we prayed twice!

The story could end happily there, but there was more. The next day, our grandson reported that his little brother had pulled a chair over to the kitchen counter and moved the Prayer Jar to the floor.

We rushed into the room fearing we'd find a broken jar. What we saw made our hearts melt. Sitting in the middle of the floor, being as gentle as he could, our tiny grandson was leaning over the open Prayer Jar, babbling his heart out to God who was definitely present with him right there in the jar!

Finally, Mary wrote a letter to her children on Mother's Day as a reminder of God's love. It very much reflects the prayer of my own heart. It reads, in part:

I must confess that so many times I have knelt in the dark of yet another day's end, begging God's forgiveness for my failures with you: my abruptness, harsh words, the ears that hear but tune out your silent pleas for understanding, the eyes that don't see the hurts of your little hearts, the omissions of simple pleasures and commissions of parental sins. I beg your forgiveness! I want to give you something this Mother's Day: a will of hope and a testament of God's love and mine.

My dear ones, I won't always be with you on the earth. You will go through crucibles of sorrows and trials. Don't allow them to defeat you! God has promised His strength to those who wait on Him. Man may fail, you may fail at times, but your loving Father will never fail you. I haven't always given you what you wanted—perhaps not even what you needed. I pray God will be the Sufficiency for my lacks, the Gentleness for my impatience, the Compassion for my misunderstandings, the Calm for my restlessness.

Dear ones, I want for you what God wants for you. He wants you to be His heroes, armed with faith, purity, and humility in a disbelieving, pleasure-seeking, vain world. God wants you to reflect His care and love to those who will cross your path of life. I thank you, dear precious gifts, for giving my life an eternal dimension—for giving me something to live, work, and strive for. You have inspired me and I love you deeply.

Teach Your Children Every Day...

Date _____

Today I commit to "bless" my children on a daily basis, thus instilling the reality that God's love for them, and the value *he* has given them, can never be taken away.

_____
Signature

■ Gary Smalley, noted family counselor, and Dr. John Trent co-wrote *The Gift of Blessing: Giving the Gift of Unconditional Love and Acceptance*, which no parent should be without. It describes the life-changing impact blessing can have on your family and fleshes out the blessing described earlier. Gary Smalley summarizes how anyone can bless any child:

"Today, as in centuries past, orthodox Jewish homes bestow a special family blessing on their children. This blessing, which is much like the patriarchal blessing Isaac bestowed upon Jacob, has been vital in providing a sense of acceptance for generations of children.

You don't need to be Jewish to value children and give them a blessing. You don't even have to be a parent. Although parents hold a responsibility to bless their children, anyone can change a child's life. They can give a child a blessing by caring enough to express acceptance, model commitment, and picture a special future. In giving children the blessing, we help insure that they will carry the heritage of love."

MORE HELP

- Brad Bright, a true leader in shaping the culture and teaching people of all ages about the high-value God places on all of us, has developed a new program just for children to help them know God. "The most important thing you can teach your children is who God really is and why it matters. Every decision they make in life will be influenced by their view of God. Discover God4Kids uses a unique, interactive approach to wrap the message of who God really is into your every day family life." Brad's many fabulous resources for parents and kids can be found at dg4kids.com.

- Mercy Ministries provides a residential counseling program free of charge to young women who have life controlling issues such as eating disorders, self-harm, unplanned pregnancy, sexual abuse, addictions and depression. The program is voluntary and lasts approximately six months. Young women receive biblically based counseling, nutrition and fitness education and life skills classes such as budgeting, setting boundaries and preparation for parenting if they are pregnant.The Mercy Ministries program takes a non-conventional approach to treatment by getting to the root issues of the problems and then helping the young women move past their debilitating circumstances, recognize and accept their self-worth and prepare them to reach their full potential. Mercy Ministries has helped over 2000 young women find freedom from very difficult issues and graduates of their program are found in universities, on the mission field, working, raising children and giving back to their communities. Visit www.mercyministries.org for more information about how to apply.

Establish A Family Tradition Of A Daily Quiet Time

THE CHALLENGE

It's hard to stay sane in a world where we are bombarded nonstop by stimuli of all variations. When your kid comes home from school, odds are he or she can choose from an iPod, cell phone, video games, computer, television, DVDs, radio, podcasts, YouTube, Facebook, My-Space, and many other modes of entertainment and distraction.

Jeffrey Brantley, an MD at Duke's Department of Psychiatry and author of *Calming Your Anxious Mind*, writes:

> Uncertainty seems to grow daily in life all around us. News-paper headlines scream of terrorist threats, international con-flict, environmental disasters, dishonesty and corruption in

government and business. Catholic priests are accused of sexual abuse. School-children are searched for weapons because some of their fellows have chosen to become mass murderers.

Life grows busier for people everywhere. Information streams at us from all directions and knows no boundary. Cell phones, pagers, voice mail, e-mail, laptop computers, and the Internet contribute to the never ending workday as people can be reached anytime, anywhere, for any reason.... Personal life can feel more and more out of control and out of balance.

Our children are growing up in a world with an unprecedented level of distractions and potential threats coming from nearly every direction. They see it in the world of their parents as well.

Blackberrys buzzing, cell phones bleeping, landlines ringing, fax machines whizzing, pagers beeping. It seems almost impossible to sit down for a family dinner, let alone make it through without one of those devices going off and calling someone away from the table. Kids want to finish eating as soon as possible to race off and watch television or get to the next level on their favorite video game.

Kids and adults need to take moments to just...breathe. Children especially need to learn the value of taking pause for reflection, as they have not yet learned how to fully grapple with the demands of everyday life.

Do you remember those care-free days of summer from your youth? Some of my fondest memories are of lying in the warm grass and just watching the clouds go by. Like many children, when I was young, I had countless opportunities to let my imagination soar. I turned those clouds into castles and animals, and wondered about the depth of the skies and universe. I delighted in the gentle breeze and smell of the fresh cut fields. It was pure magic—peaceful and inspiring.

My favorite place in the world is the beach—and growing up in Florida, I had many blessed opportunities to walk long stretches of an island shore in solitude. It was in these moments that I thought about the many blessings in life, let my mind absorb the beauty around me, and began to form words and thoughts into the poems and stories of my heart. I started taking a notebook with me when I was in the fourth grade and often sat near the sandy dunes and wrote. I still have some of the poetry I composed in those early years, and today, writing is one of my most therapeutic activities. I am convinced that many of the skills I developed came as a result of my parents encouraging me to "be still."

One of the most powerful bible verses is Psalm 46:10, "Be still and know that I am God."

It is in the quiet moments of our lives that God reveals himself most intimately to us. If we meditate on and consider his words in our place of solitude, our faith begins to soar and we can sense his presence. How many teens do you know that say they have felt a closeness with God? If they spend all their time in frantic activity or watching television, then although they may be good kids, chances are that they may never have experienced a Divine, personal connection.

Making daily quiet times a part of your home can bring benefits to the physical and mental well-being of everyone. Quiet times also offer the opportunity to bond more deeply with your family as you master the art of simply spending time together. And quiet times don't have to be silent—they are often most powerful when they are filled with our sincere prayers to the living God.

IN YOUR SHOES

Alice, a reader from New York City, wrote to me about her own experience with enforced quiet times as a child and their impact on her adult life:

Quiet times were something my parents emphasized from an early age. They used to frustrate me, because I was always very fidgety as a child. I wanted to spend my free time running around, playing games, singing, playing with other children, and other wild, boisterous activities. But every day, my parents would make me spend an hour of quiet time. I had to spend the first thirty minutes lying down. If I did not fall asleep, then I could spend the remaining thirty minutes doing something still and quiet in my room. Ninety-five percent of the time, I spent the remaining thirty minutes reading.

A few things happened as a result, but I did not notice them until I was an adult. First, I developed a deep-seated passion for reading. Spending that thirty minutes a day reading got me hooked. Often, I would enjoy my book so much that I would read it longer than the required thirty minutes. That love for reading has extended into my adult life. Living a busy and fast paced life in New York City, this time spent alone reading is a little gem buried in the rough of day-to-day life. When I am feeling anxious or overwhelmed, I know that just picking up something to read will relax me. I think that association between calmness and reading stems all the way back from my regular habit of quiet time and reading in my youth. I have noticed that most of my peers do not have the same love for reading, and they were not required to spend time being quiet as children. I think the link is definitely there.

In addition to developing a love for reading, I learned the simple art of clearing my head in the middle of the day. Even when I do not "feel" stressed, I am often amazed at how spending some time with the TV off, in silence, will give me a great sense of refreshment. It's like letting your mind take a nap. Sometimes our minds are so jumbled that they don't even know how to tell us to give it a rest for a few minutes.

Establish a Family Tradition of a Daily Quiet Time

The habit of calming my mind daily began in childhood, so I learned from an early age the necessity of taking just a little bit of time, and the difference it can make during the day. Even in college, I made a big point of taking at least 30 minutes to myself. Sometimes I would walk down to the nearby coffee shop and people watch or read. Other times I would go to the quiet room of the library with a magazine. People thought I was crazy to do this during busy times like finals, but the only thing that got me through those stressful periods was taking a little "time out."

One reader and mother of five, Leslie, recently wrote to me about how her family established a time for reflection after dinner, and how it changed her family for the better:

My family grew up eating dinner together six nights a week. I knew that this was a highly uncommon practice in the American social landscape, but I cherished it. After all the craziness of each school day, sports practices, theatre and choir practice, scrimmages, and the like, my kids would come tumbling into the house and we would sit down, pray, and eat together.

That worked until my oldest kids got into their late teenage years. They began staying late at school, heading out with their friends, and needing to skip dinner to study. Our family dinners began to fall apart. My youngest boys also began to play video games and spend more time on the computer. As soon as they finished shoveling food down their throats they would jump up and ask to be excused and race downstairs. After awhile, I grew exasperated and gave up trying to keep everyone in their seats.

One night, after spending an hour preparing dinner, one child showed up at the dinner table. My husband was in his office working, two children were at school, one was out with a friend, and another was still playing sports with the neighbor kids despite being told what time we would sit down.

I decided that enough was enough.

The following night I told each member of my family that if they wanted to eat anything at all the next night, they would be at dinner for an important announcement, otherwise the kitchen would close shortly afterwards, and they would be unable to eat.

The next night I told my family that we had to start working towards spending some time together. I told them that I understood that it could not be every night. I understood that everyone has important commitments. But commitment to family should be the number one priority.

I proposed that every person commit to dinner with the family four nights a week. That commitment included staying at the table for thirty full minutes, followed by fifteen minutes of reading, silence, or quiet discussion in the living room. We could tell each other about our days, read the newspaper together, or read a Scripture passage and discuss it for ten minutes. Anything.

It was hard but it worked. Now my three oldest are off at college, but I feel like for the rest of their time in my house, they spend more time just unwinding at the end of each day and getting to spend some quality time with their family. I treasured those quiet moments with them after dinner, and am so glad I had the chance to know them a little better and teach them the value of reflection and family before they left to go out into the world.

FROM MY HOME TO YOURS

Here are just a few tips for creating successful quiet times at your home. Since every family is unique, you should evaluate yours and sit down to discuss how you can carve out time for reflection. Sometimes our teens and kids feel so much pressure to be busy that they just might find it refreshing to know that you believe they need time to relax.

- ❏ Create a monthly chart with a spot to record the amount of time spent in silence each day and what "quiet" activity was done during the time.
- ❏ Have a list on hand of ways to spend quality time in silence, such as "Everyone reads a book" or "Go for a walk."
- ❏ Make prayer a part of your quiet time.
- ❏ Have each member in your family keep a journal for their thoughts during quiet time.
- ❏ Make sure you have a "space" that is conducive to reflection. A room with no tempting electronic devices is ideal. Make sure you have a place that is comfortable for sitting and relaxing.
- ❏ When you plan family vacations and outings, choose places that offer both activity and lovely natural surroundings.
- ❏ Purchase a family devotional like the small one you can get each month called "Our Daily Bread" (Published by RBC Ministries, it is available at RBC.org). This publication includes a small passage and thought to meditate on for each day of the month. Reading it at the start of a family quiet time will enable you to plant seeds of truth and thought in the minds of your kids that they can then nurture through reflection and prayer after the reading is over.

ACT NOW

Date _____

Today my family and I began having "quiet" time. I also pledged to set the example by being "still and reflective" and encouraging my family to do the same.

_____
Signature

MORE HELP

Certain Peace in Uncertain Times is a moving book by Shirley Dobson that will help teach you the power and peace of prayer. Mrs. Dobson reminds us that the God of the Universe desires to hear from us—and that His peace awaits those who call on him. As Mrs. Dobson points out, "Yet God does not abandon us. He keeps His promise: 'Never will I leave you; never will I forsake you.' (Hebrews 13:5). Even during the storms, He stands just to the side, ever watchful, waiting to embrace us the moment we again seek His presence. His words to Jeremiah apply to us all: 'Call to me and I will answer you.' (Jeremiah 33:3)."

Set The Example

THE CHALLENGE

We all know stories of bad parents.

We hear about mothers who criticize teachers for daring to give their little darlings a failing grade and about fathers who scream obscenities at umpires from the sidelines of a Little League baseball game. Perhaps we've even witnessed such incidents ourselves. All around us are parents behaving in a rude and crass manner that would have been deemed unthinkable a generation or two ago. We shake our heads and wonder what the world is coming to.

But before we point the finger of blame, let's ask ourselves: are we good models for our children—and other people's children, for that matter?

It's not enough to simply refrain from the flagrantly bad behavior listed above. That, quite frankly, sets the standard far too low. I'm starting from the assumption that you're not acting like some substance-abusing celebrity mother who has just had her parenting techniques dissected in the supermarket tabloids. No, you're a mother or father who works hard, at home and on the job, and you truly want what's best for your children.

And what do they need—besides food, clothes, shelter, and all the material things we strive after so mightily, day after day? They need you to provide a good example. And you do that primarily with your actions.

We've all heard the old adage, "Do as I say, not as I do." Of course, the reason that's a joke is precisely because you can't expect a child to do that at all. If anything, it's the opposite—if your actions don't match your words, they'll ignore the latter, no matter how carefully you couch your "pearls of wisdom." As Ralph Waldo Emerson once said, "What you do speaks so loudly that I cannot hear what you say."

Show me a child who doesn't interrupt, for example. I guarantee you that his parents haven't simply said, "Don't interrupt—it isn't nice." That child has seen his parents listen patiently when other people are talking, and he has learned to model their good behavior. Show me a teenager who is generous, and I know to expect the same trait from her mother and father, who—and this is a crucial point—may not even realize that they're being watched and copied.

What we've got to keep in mind is that they *are* watching—and learning, for good or for ill. They watch our interactions with others and our reactions. For instance, when they hear us refuse to listen to a dirty joke, that makes an impression. When we watch our language, they do likewise. When we lose a game graciously, they're learning how to react when the same thing happens to them.

Obviously—perhaps unfortunately, given our fallen human nature—the same principle applies when we model bad behavior. Take driving, for instance. State Farm insurance company released a study in September 2008 showing that most teenagers report seeing their parents drive in an unsafe manner. More than two-thirds said their parents were speeding, talking on their cell phones, and/or driving while tired. If you're one of these teenagers, what are you going to think when your parents turn around and give you a big lecture about safe driving?

I'm not suggesting that you have to be perfect. We all make mistakes from time to time. But remember, children learn from what they see and hear you doing day in and day out. They pick up on *patterns*. So we've got to try our best to make those patterns worth emulating.

That can be quite a challenge in a culture that celebrates childish and boorish behavior. In movies, books, and TV shows, today's "stars" prefer impulse to self-control. "Everywhere I turn today, I see men who refuse to grow up," writes Gary Cross, a history professor at Pennsylvania State University, in the book, *Men to Boys: The Making of Modern Immaturity*. "Boys used to have leading men such as John Wayne and James Stewart to look up to. Now they've got Adam Sandler and Will Ferrell. We don't have clean-cut crooners just hoping to hold a girl's hand, we've got rockers and rappers with far more carnal desires— and they're not shy about telling everyone, often in filthy language."

You must set a good example. Your children are looking to you for guidance, whether you—or they—even realize it. If you're not already taking that responsibility seriously, now's the time to start.

The good news is that common sense will take you a good part of the way here. Most parents instinctively modify their behavior when children come along. But others don't realize that even the smallest of children will start copying their behavior. One of my friends is a teacher and she said that she can tell by a student's language whose parents use foul words at home, and whose don't. She also knows which parents model good manners—and which ones don't. Of this you can be certain: your child will tell on you. Maybe not literally, but their attitudes and actions will reflect what they see and hear. And no matter how good or wholesome you are, if they consume rotten media messages, their lives will model that, too. You have to work extra hard to model good behavior for your kids because you are up against a culture of garbage that is trying to influence them to behave like garbage too.

FROM MY HOME TO YOURS

Nearly all of us can use a little help beyond these basics. After all, we're aiming for something higher: to turn the next generation into men and women of pride and accomplishment and to help them become the people that God intends for them to be. To that end, I have a few suggestions:

Always model honesty and truth. There is no difference between a "little white lie" and a "big fat lie" and our kids know it. If you are dishonest in your speech or actions—even a "tad bit"—you are modeling complete dishonesty for your children. You are teaching them to practice situational ethics versus absolute honesty. Speaking truth and being a person of integrity in all that you do is the right way to live, but it will also have a tremendous impact on your son or daughter and how they treat others. Doing otherwise is not only wrong; it can cause mass confusion in a child's developing sense of morality. It's very frustrating to a child for you to punish them for telling you a lie if they have seen or heard you be less than honest with your friends or them. Always be true and faithful in word and deed, and your children will respect you, trust you, and grow up to emulate you.

Speak up when you see or hear something wrong. When you encounter something that offends your values, don't simply look the other way. Let your child know how you feel and why. I'm not saying that you should always be ready to launch into a lecture—just a word or two will usually do. If you're passing one of those soft-porn Victoria's Secret displays at the mall, for instance, shake your head and say something

Set the Example

like, "I can't believe they'd want to show pictures of women half-naked in public. That's just wrong." The same principle applies when you run across bad movies or TV shows. Don't just assume they'll understand something is wrong. They're looking for guidance. Provide it.

Let your kids see you reading good material. Children and teens notice what their parents read. Every time you pick up a trashy magazine at the grocery store check-out stand or in the waiting room at the dentist's office, they notice. If you read one of those popular (and mindless) romance novels, chances are that your daughter has picked it up when you weren't looking and read parts of it, too. Look for quality books of history, faith, and fiction and make it a point to let your kids see you reading them.

Show good sportsmanship. Whatever activities your family enjoys, from softball games to touch football, from Monopoly to Scrabble, teach your kids how to win and how to lose. A good winner doesn't gloat (although a little good-natured ribbing is okay), and a good loser doesn't pitch a fit, but is gracious and congratulates the winner.

Be a good listener. If you're always lecturing instead of listening, chances are your kids will avoid having these one-way conversations with you. Your kids should know that they can always talk to you about what's on their minds. Ask questions that get them started, avoid immediate negative reactions, and try to make it natural. (In other words, don't just sit at the table and say you want to talk; ask them to help you with dinner and engage them in conversation while they're filling the glasses with ice.) When you listen to them, they will learn to listen to you!

When you make a mistake, apologize. There's nothing wrong with saying, "Honey, I'm sorry I lost my temper like that." That itself sets a good example, reminding them that they shouldn't let pride interfere with doing what's right.

Don't whine! Ok, so I said it. Parents (especially moms) can get so frustrated with the pains and annoyances of everyday life that before we know it, we have turned into Wendy Whiner. Be bold and vocal about what is wrong—and then work to change it if you can. But never, ever, endlessly whine and complain around your kids. If you do—you absolutely will get massive amounts of whining in return.

Learn to forgive—and forget. Nothing will destroy a human being faster than bitterness. Harboring resentment and anger also robs us of the opportunity to enjoy life and its many beautiful moments. Your children *will* be harmed by many people in their lives, and how they learn to deal with it depends largely on you. When you are betrayed, or tricked, or hurt in any way, it's critical for you to seek justice, practice forgiveness, and then move on. Dwelling on the mistakes of others not only zaps you of energy, it can cause your child to wonder if you will ever really forgive them when they do something wrong. Teaching your son or daughter to forgive and forget will free them from the future bondage of bitterness and vengefulness.

Mind your manners. Need I say more? Probably. Always practice kindness and thoughtfulness—open the door for others, go out of your way to be helpful, and for goodness sake, mind your manners!

Be generous. Regardless of financial circumstances, everyone can be generous with something. Ours is a materialistic, selfish society where each person is taught to fend for himself. Show your kids that you don't wait for the government to tax you to help others—you give freely of your blessings. Whether it is money, time, kindness, or displaying a cheerful spirit, show your teen by your daily life how important it is to give.

Set the Example

MORE HELP

- Focus on the Family (family.org): This wonderful organization, run by the terrific Dr. James Dobson, has many helpful resources for parents. The "Parenting" section on its Web site carries a wealth of good information for time-strapped mothers and fathers, from "effective Biblical discipline" to "your child's emotions." They also offer many good articles, videos, books, and publications such as "The Strong-Willed Child" and "Raising Respectful Children in a Disrespectful World."

- *Stop Whining, Start Living*: I love Dr. Laura Schlessinger. She really tells it like it is and is never afraid to challenge parents to stand up and be the parents! In this terrific book she reminds us that whining and complaining will not bring about change in our lives or families—it's only when we take action that change comes. I believe one of the greatest skills a parent can master is the art of **not** whining or complaining endlessly about their kids and their behavior. Dr. Laura's book is a great place to start in learning how to master your own life, and then modeling for your kids every day the type of character and attitude it takes to live life to its fullest. If you take Dr. Laura's advice to heart, you will have a more fulfilled life— and you will naturally become a powerful example for your kids.

continued

MORE HELP

- *Strong Fathers, Strong Daughters: 10 Secrets Every Father Should Know,* this book by Dr. Meg Meeker, a teen health expert, is one that every father with daughters ought to read. Chapters include: "She Needs a Hero," "Be the Man You Want Her to Marry," and "Protect Her, Defend Her (and use a shotgun if necessary)." It's loaded with good advice for fathers who want to counteract the insidious and disgraceful way that modern radical feminism has tried to exclude the most important man in every girl's life.

Follow Ten Simple Steps With Your Teens To Foster Ongoing Support For Their Purity

THE CHALLENGE

We live in a culture that is saturated in sex.

Store in the malls sell t-shirts advertising promiscuity with writing such as "Everyone Loves a Slutty Girl" sprawled across the chest. An internet search for "slutty t-shirts" returns close to a million hits for online stores selling degrading tops.

Television shows like "Sex and the City" and "Lipstick Jungle" bombard young women with the idea that for today's "modern woman," men and sex go together like a pair of expensive heels and city sidewalks.

Sexuality today has been reduced to little more than an amusing hobby, and the concept of sexual purity has come to be thought of as backwards and outdated. In fact, today's culture teaches that "self-respect" and sexual "liberation" (a nicer word for promiscuity), go hand-in-hand.

Wendy Shalit, author of *A Return to Modesty: Discovering the Lost Virtue* noted that Naomi Wolf wrote in her latest novel that "there are no good girls; we are all bad girls," and that we all should just admit it and "explore the shadow slut who walks alongside us."

Ms. Shalit continued, "We certainly feel the pressure and get the message that we are supposed to be bad—we, after all, started our sex education in elementary school—but when everyone is saying the same thing, it makes us wonder: isn't there anything more to life, to love?"

Our sons and daughters alike are growing up asking this very question. And the answer that society gives them could not be more wrong, or more dangerous.

Shalit writes further that "the woes besetting the modern young woman—sexual harassment, stalking, rape, even 'whirlpooling' (when a group of guys surround a girl who is swimming, and then sexually assault her)—are all expressions of a society which has lost its respect for female modesty."

What are you teaching your daughter about the origin of her self-worth and the value of her purity? What are you teaching your son about his?

The bottom line is that you are your son's and daughter's first and last line of defense against the sexual pressures that are closing in around them. You can't rely on the schools to do it. As a matter of fact, much of the "abstinence based" curriculum in schools today is exactly the opposite. The vast majority of comprehensive sex education teaches our children to think sexual activity is fine, as long as they can handle it. You owe it to your son and daughter to actually take the time to read their sex education materials. You might just be shocked at what you find.

Follow Ten Simple Steps with Your Teens...

As a culture, we have lost appreciation for the virtue of modesty and chastity. Many scientific and sociological studies are emerging that demonstrate the physical and psychological harms resulting from young women abandoning the virtue of chastity.

The American Psychological Association recently released a seventy-two page report on the damaging effects of the sexualization of our children. The study asserts that sexualization occurs when:

- a person's value comes only from his or her sexual appeal or behavior, to the exclusion of other characteristics;
- a person is held to a standard that equates physical attractiveness (narrowly defined) with being sexy;
- a person is sexually objectified—that is, made into a thing for others' sexual use, rather than seen as a person with the capacity for independent action and decision making; and/or
- sexuality is inappropriately imposed upon a person.

  All four conditions need not be present; any one is an indication of sexualization.

Our children are undeniably saturated in all four methods of sexualization in nearly every aspect of culture, ranging from schools to shopping malls.

The statistics demonstrating the rise in harmful and objectifying behavior in recent years are endless and alarming. Here are just a few tidbits:

- According to the American Psychological Association, just between the years of 2002 and 2003, the number of young women under age eighteen who received breast implants tripled.

- The National Center for Disease Control and Prevention reports that 46.8 percent of all high school students claim they have had sexual intercourse. 6.2 percent of those same students had had sexual intercourse with four or more persons during their life.

- The National Campaign to Prevent Teen Pregnancy reports that the United States currently has the highest rates of teen pregnancy and births in the Western industrialized world. The report finds that approximately three in ten women under the age of 20 will become pregnant.

- A 2005 study by the American Social Health Association found that fifty percent of sexually active youth age twenty-five and younger will contract a sexually-transmitted disease.

Need I say more?

But here is the clincher: a study done by the National Campaign to Prevent Teen Pregnancy found that a majority of both girls and boys who are sexually active wish they had waited. Of those who have had sex, more than one half of teen boys (55 percent) and the majority of teen girls (70 percent) said they wish they had waited to have sex.

Mom, dad—your kids need your active involvement to help keep them from having such regrets. Your influence must not be underestimated. Just read these personal stories and see how much impact you can have on your teens:

IN YOUR SHOES

This comes from a dear friend and former colleague, Rebekah Coons. She is an amazing twenty-something woman whose wisdom, faith, and strong moral convictions astound me daily.

Follow Ten Simple Steps with Your Teens...

When I read this story about her father, I suddenly knew why she is such a remarkable person:

My dad was very influential in my life from as long as I can remember. From sharing his personal faith, to reading my three sisters and me Bible stories as we fell to sleep at night, he was slowly but consistently making little character investments in us that would pay off the rest of our lives. The biggest deposit my dad made in my life was when I turned thirteen years old.

Dad asked me out on a 'special daddy-daughter date night' and asked me 'dress up' because we were going to a fancy restaurant. Needless to say, I felt like a princess...the evening couldn't have been more magical. During dinner we talked about my birthday and how excited I was about becoming a teenager. He mostly let me do all the talking and quietly guided the conversation to the topic of boys and love towards the end of our meal. As we were discussing the subject, the waiter quietly interrupted us and presented me with a silver tray which had a small, wrapped box sitting in the middle of it. It was a gift from my dad. I unwrapped it and opened the box to find a poem and a gold heart locket and key necklace. The poem stated how much he and my heavenly Father loved me and how important it was to remain pure for my future husband, a man who will vow to love, cherish and protect my heart for the rest of my life. Until I met that man, dad would guard the key to my heart and protect me.

Fast forward ten years, I graduated college with the key and locket still around my neck. I will never forget my dad's words save yourself for your husband, a man who will vow to love, cherish and protect you for the rest of your life.

Not long after graduation, it came time to give my key away. It was my wedding day, and as an ordained minister, my Dad conducted the ceremony. After leading us in our vows, it came time for dad to make his second presentation of the heart and key necklace, except this time, he left the heart with me. He said:

'We are so proud of you. The Bible says it like this, 'I have no greater joy than to hear that my children are walking in truth (3 John 4). The two of you from the outset of your relationship have wanted to honor the Lord and honor each other. Keep this as your number one goal and it will serve you well throughout your marriage.'

With a tear in his eye my dad presented my new husband with the key to my heart.

At that moment it hit me: my dad had been preparing me for this moment since my thirteenth birthday. Honoring the Lord by remaining pure until marriage was merely laying the solid foundation for a marriage that is being built to last a lifetime.

Recently I was talking with a beautiful teenage girl I know. We were discussing what motivates her to remain sexually pure. She said it was, simply, "My sense of morality, which is based on my faith and the values my mother and father have taught me." This young woman is very active in her church and her parents have always been very frank in their discussions with her about sex, abstinence, and wanting the very best for her life. It was exciting and encouraging to hear that her parents and faith have more influence on this young woman than even massive amounts of media that glorify sexual promiscuity! When I asked her what the second reason is for her decision to remain chaste, she said, "Respect. I know that I will have more respect from my peers if I uphold high standards."

So there you have it in a nutshell. Morality, faith, and the values that we as parents pass on to our kids, along with the need to be respected, can provide all the protection our children need in this hyper-sexed world. This is the recipe for teaching our children how to remain sexually pure until marriage. If you think this young woman is an anomaly, think again.

In study after study, when asked what influences them the most, teenagers say.... their parents. Even though our kids are consuming some $6^1/_2$ hours of media a day, they still say their parents have the greatest impact on them. So the point here isn't whether or not you have an influence, mom and dad. The question is, "How are you going to use it?" Your silence on issues of sexual activity will be taken as an endorsement of the status quo. But your active involvement and discussions with your teens on the subject can be the greatest force for good.

One outstanding young woman I know, Ashley Samelson, graduated from Tufts University—which, like most colleges today—is a hotbed of liberalism. Her senior year, she stumbled across a "sex-fair" on Valentine's Day. Disgusted, she wrote a piece for her school newspaper. The following are excerpts:

> On Valentine's Day I made the mistake of walking through the campus center. I imagined there would be people selling flowers that one could buy for a friend or sweetheart, chocolates, kiss-o-grams, candy hearts—all things related to love, friendship, or kindness, values the world understands Valentine's Day to celebrate. What I discovered instead was a disgrace...

As a female, but also as a human being, the sex fair held in the name of 'feminism' and 'education' was insulting and disturbing. It was disconcerting to see on Valentine's Day, of all days, that meaningless sexual pleasure appears to have replaced any concept of love and respect...

Buckets of condoms, sex toys, sex games, genitalia cookies and masturbation tables sent the message that sex is virtually meaningless, something to joke about, and that sexual awareness comes through learning to be free and detached mentally and emotionally by ridding oneself of any moral and emotional barriers that may accompany sex...

Encouraging women to be free and casual with their sex (so long as it's 'safe') sends the message to men that women are available as sexual objects, merely instruments for obtaining meaningless pleasure. If women are careless and emotion-free about sex, why should they be treated with any care at all?

Both men and women need to learn that casual sex is emotionally damaging... and is neither liberating nor fulfilling. Re-teaching love, respect, and reverence is the first step towards... restoring chivalry in men and true awareness and self-esteem in women.

Her inbox was flooded with positive responses. She said that for days, young women showed up at the door of her dorm room, shyly agreeing that they, too, wished there was greater respect for chastity on campus, some tearfully telling stories of some promiscuous encounter that had left them feeling lonely and empty.

Don't let your daughter or son become a sexual statistic by following these practical tips:

Follow Ten Simple Steps with Your Teens...

❑ Have frequent discussions and give gentle reminders to your children about how sex was created by God for marriage.

❑ Nurture a culture of openness in your home where they can feel comfortable coming to you with questions about their developing sexuality.

❑ Filter out any publications or media that treat women like sex objects or glorify promiscuity.

❑ Go through an age-appropriate program on abstinence education with your pre-teen and/or teenager (See Even More Help for suggestions)

❑ Encourage group activities versus couple dating.

❑ Make your home the place where kids hang out.

❑ Keep your teenagers active in sports, volunteer activities, church, work, or better yet—with you.

❑ Monitor where they go, and who they hang out with. As long as your teen lives under your roof, you have the responsibility and right to know where they are.

❑ Opt your kids and teens out of the graphic sex education taught in many public schools. (Call your local school to learn how—but don't let them discourage you.)

❑ Find a strong faith-based or church-based youth group and encourage your teen to become involved. (Young Life (younglife.org) is a fantastic organization for high school students. You can access their website to find a group near you.)

ACT NOW

Date _____

    Today I pledged that I will be bold in passing on the value of sexual purity to my children, and will foster an atmosphere that helps them overcome the cultural pressures.

_____
Signature

MORE HELP

Thankfully, there is now a world of excellent abstinence materials for you and your sons and daughters. Three of the best sites for all kinds of resources are:

- The Abstinence Clearinghouse (abstinenceclearinghouse.com)

- Focus on the Family (family.org)
  (NOTE: they offer excellent teen magazines for both guys and girls)

Just of a few of the great books for guys and girls are:

- *Why Wait?* by Josh McDowell's best-seller

- *For Young Women Only* by Shaunti Feldham and Lisa A. Rice
  (NOTE: this book is absolutely perfect for teenage girls.)

- *Passion and Purity* by Elizabeth Elliott

- *Secret Keeper* by Dannah Gresh

Set Clothing Standards For Your Daughter That Reflect She Is To Be Respected And Admired For Who She Truly Is

THE CHALLENGE

Today's little girls are dressing like street-walkers. It used to be a father's greatest privilege to protect his daughter's virtue. Yet, dads across America are allowing their innocent young daughters—many as young as seven or eight—to dress in a manner that degrades them, over-sexualizes their image, and portrays them as nothing more than an object to be used. Mothers are driving their little girls to the mall and plunking down big bucks for thongs, and tight pants and little tops that reveal their bottoms and hip bones. Have we gone mad? Face the facts: most 12–16-year-olds don't have access to a lot of cash—unless their parents give it to them. And, last I heard, in most states if you're below the age of siteen you simply can't hop in a car and drive yourself to the local mall. Nope, it's not the kids' money that is being spent, it's their parents'. And it's usually the mom that happily drives the little darlings to the mall for a fun day of shopping.

Face it: little girls dress according to what their mommies allow. I thought mothers were supposed to model virtue for their daughters, to teach them to value themselves and their bodies. What chance does a little girl stand of keeping her childhood or innocence intact when it's mommy that's driving her to the store and paying for the thongs, the itty-bitty skirts, the hipster jeans, and the plunging necklines?

A 2007 study by the American Psychological Association entitled, "Report of the APA Task Force on the Sexualization of Girls" reveals the harms of treating our young daughters as sex objects. The report says, in part:

> [S]exualization [is linked] to a variety of harmful consequences. These consequences include harm to the sexualized individuals themselves, to their interpersonal relationships, and to society. For example, there is evidence that sexualization contributes to impaired cognitive performance in college-aged women, and related research suggests that viewing material that is sexually objectifying can contribute to body dissatisfaction, eating disorders, low self-esteem, depressive affect, and even physical health problems in high-school-aged girls and in young women. The sexualization of girls may not only reflect sexist attitudes, a societal tolerance of sexual violence, and the exploitation of girls and women but may also contribute to these phenomena.

That should be enough for any parent to regain their common sense—it's just plain dumb to dress our little girls in ways that degrade them. Refuse to allow the mass marketers to define your daughter's value. Let your daughter know, in loving but uncompromising terms, what clothing will and will not be acceptable.

IN YOUR SHOES

Our daughters need to understand that they are all beautiful creations of value. They need to know that they are to be respected, and should be judged by their character and kindness and who they are on the inside. They need to understand that they can be tasteful and still look fabulous. The conversation I have had several times with my teen daughter about clothing goes something like this: "Kristin, God made you lovely and special. You are someone to be respected. And I, as your mom—the one who loves you more than anyone else in the world could possible love you, and who deeply understands the need and desire to feel attractive—commit to you that I'm going to help make sure that you dress in a way that shows your inner character, reveals your true beauty, individuality, and the fact that you are not just a toy. So, we'll have only one rule before we buy something: we both have to like it. That's it. That means that you won't try and convince me to buy an item that I think is inappropriate. And it also means that I will not to try and force you to wear something that you think is dorky."

Guess what? This method works. Yes, I have had to repeat it several times as the new shopping seasons and styles arrive. And yes, my daughter and I have shed a few tears of stress during unfruitful shopping trips. And, of course, we've often been tempted after a long day of trudging from store to store to give in. But we don't. We don't because my daughter and I know that our values don't change with the trends or when we're tired or when some designer in NY lowers the bar (yet again). And each time we uphold our standards instead of the shifting standards of the world, my daughter is reminded of her true value and of my undying love for her.

It's not easy for anyone, even my daughter and me. Despite her keen sense of morality, Kristin is still a teenager, subject to the pressures of our modern toxic culture:

One day, we were shopping for swimwear and shorts for our summer vacation. But the last two hours of the trip almost made me want to bag the whole vacation. If you don't have young girls, then you probably can't understand the dilemma. It's quite simple, really. The problem is that there are virtually no swimsuits, tops or shorts designed for tweens and teens that don't resemble something a streetwalker would wear. As a capitalist, I find it very strange that an entire segment of the American population is so underserved—very strange indeed. Most of the moms and dads I know are thoroughly frustrated with the poor selection of clothing, but in the end, shrug their shoulders, cast aside their best judgment, and purchase the teeny weenie bikinis for their innocent young daughters anyway.

We tried on item after item, hoping against hope that maybe the next pair of shorts would actually come up somewhere near her naval, or that the next bathing suit wouldn't really be as tiny and revealing as it looked on the hanger. But time after time, I had to shake my head and say, 'no.' Which is why tears started to well up in Kristin's beautiful green eyes.

For a moment, I thought of ignoring the reddening eyes as we continued our mission to find something decent. But I thought better of it, sigh, and simply, softly said, 'Sweetheart' as I stepped forward and hugged her close. This act of under-

standing was enough to send the pooled waters spilling down her cheeks. We remained in our silent embrace for several minutes and then I stepped back and wiped away her tears. She sweetly smiled as I said, 'We'll keep on looking—no matter how long it takes—until we find something you like, and that also reflects the honor and respect for your body that you deserve.'

Later, with only two items that pass muster—as I'm putting the hangers on the dozens of items that didn't work— Kristin came to me. She put her arms around my neck and said, 'I'm sorry I was being so difficult.' Again, she shed a few tears, and I marveled at the incredible gift, privilege, and responsibility of being a mother.

'Kristin,' I said, 'You weren't difficult at all. I'm sorry you live in a world where so many adults have failed in their responsibility to treat children like the treasures you are. Thanks for allowing me to be the mom, Kristin. The mom who loves you more than anyone in the world could possibly love you. The mom who wants what is best for you.' She stepped back, looked directly in my eyes, and said, 'I love you, mommy.'

We left the store a bit more determined to fight for our values, a bit more disgusted that there has to be a battle at all, and a lot closer to each other. All in all, it was day I will long remember and even come to cherish as a reminder that fighting the culture is sometimes frustrating and exhausting, but always, always worth the effort.

Your daughters are looking to you for direction and protection. Your little girls want you to set loving standards, to let them know they are of value. And there isn't anyone else that's going to do it. Our culture has sold our daughters short—will you be guilty of it too?

You can fight back, however. A few years ago, a story written by Nick Perry of the Seattle Times caught my attention. It shows just how much impact one little girl can have in the culture war. The article read, in part:

A letter from eleven-year-old Ella Gunderson reached the retailer's executives, who promise fashions for young customers wanting more fabric over their skin. Ella Gunderson became frustrated trying to find something fashionable—yet modest—in a world where she seems to be surrounded by low-riding jeans and tight, revealing tops. So she penned a letter.'Dear Nordstrom,' she wrote. 'I am an eleven-year-old girl who has tried shopping at your store for clothes (in particular jeans), but all of them ride way under my hips, and the next size up is too big and falls down.' I see all of these girls who walk around with pants that show their belly button and underwear,' she wrote. 'Your clearks sugjest that there is only one look. If that is true, then girls are suppost to walk around half naked. I think that you should change that.' (sic)Ella's letter was relayed all the way up to Pete Nordstrom, an executive vice president and president of Nordstrom's full-line stores. Two Nordstrom executives wrote back, promising the Redmond girl the company would try to educate both its purchasing managers and salespeople on the range of fashion choices that should be available to young people. 'Wow,' wrote back Kris Allan, manager of Nordstrom's Bellevue Square store, where Ella shopped. 'Your letter really got my attention...I think you are absolutely right. There should not be just one look for everyone. This look is not particularly a modest one and there should be choices for everyone.'

Just think what you and a few friends and your daughters could do to change your local store's clothing choices!

Set Clothing Standards for Your Daughter...

MORE HELP

You aren't alone! Thousands of families are going through the same thing. So don't give up. And don't despair—there are modest alternatives. Some readers of my Townhall.com column recommend *Lands' End* and *L.L. Bean*, both of which feature one-piece suits and "tankinis." Two companies I really love are, *Modest By Design* ("clothing your father would approve of") and ShadeClothing.com. PureFashion.com is also a tremendous resource. Pure Fashion even sponsors fashion shows in many of cities across the country that uplift—rather than degrade—the value of young women. There are many others resources, too. As one reader of my column said, "If you Google 'modest swimsuits,' you'll find literally thousands of options."

Another great resource for your daughter is the book, *Dressing with Dignity* by former model Colleen Hammond. Colleen offers positive reinforcement about how men and boys treat girls who dress themselves with respect differently than they do those who dress as if all they have to offer the world is their sexual organs: "I believe it is because, subconsciously, men can read women's body language. If they see a woman who dresses

continued

with dignity and carries herself with grace and femininity, they pick up on that. They take it as a sign to approach her with the respect, reverence and honor a woman ought to have."

Finally, you must read the story of former Super-Model Kim Alexis. She is a delightful person and freely shares her spiritual journey in her fantastic book, *A Model for a Better Future.* Kim has graced the covers of hundreds of magazines over the years and continues to be one of the most beautiful women in the world. But she is lovely on the inside, too. I once had the pleasure of sharing a room with her on a women's retreat and found that her true beauty lies in her heart for the nation's young women.

One very candid admission Kim makes in her book about her modeling career is, "The worst part of this business is that you are constantly asked to compromise your moral standards. There are pictures I look back on today and think, Oh, why did I let them talk me into that? I made some choices I'm not proud of." Kim tells us, "Many women are playing with fire in the way they dress. Dressing like a floozy tells the world. 'Look at me, want me, lust after me. I'm easy and you can have me.' Displaying intimate parts of the body is a form of advertising for sex—so if you dress to attract sexual attention, you can hardly blame anyone else if that kind of attention comes your way."

"Dressing modestly tells the world, 'I respect myself and I insist on being treated with respect.'" Kim says.

So what's the one simple rule I've learned works when it's time to go shopping with my daughter? It's actually very effective, so I offer it to you again, "We both have to like it." Problem solved. When you set the standards and stick with them, while leaving room for trendy new fashions that you may not like—but that don't violate your values—you can actually have fun shopping and bond with your daughter in the process.

Dress Your Son
In Respect

THE CHALLENGE

Let's face it, chivalry in young men is hard to come by these days. Radical feminism has taught us that door-holding and other such genteel behavior are part of "rigid gender roles" that should just be thrown out the door. And to further erode civility, just look at how young boys are taught to behave by the mass media. What you get is a generation of young males who are confused or have no idea how they are supposed to treat young women or their elders. Battling a culture that devalues civility and purposefully attacks tradition makes it nearly impossible to teach our sons to be gentlemen. One of the most eye-opening videos I've ever seen, *Merchants of Cool* (produced by PBS) carefully documents why and how the modern media robs young males of their dignity. The marketing industry deliberately cultivates a grotesque male image known as a "mook"—their definition of modern teen boys. As I described in "Understand How Marketers Target Your Children," programmers have discovered that the best way to increase viewer-ship among teen boys is by showing rude, crude behavior by other boys. It also reinforces the behavior as normal, acceptable—even desirable—for our nation's young men.

The bottom line is the bottom dollar: Those who market to our teens seek to manipulate their raw emotions, and prey on their raging sexual curiosity and the natural confusion in identity and insecurity that comes in the teen years—all in order to boost ratings and make money. In her book *The War Against Boys*, Christina Hoff Summers documents the moral fallout that has occurred in the wake of the decline of respectful young men. She tells countless stories, including the story of Tawnya Brady, a high-school student in Petaluma, California. When Tawnya would walk down the hallways of her school, her male peers would actually "moo" at her, a crude reference to the size of her breasts. Ms. Summers writes, "Examples such as these, which are not rare—strongly suggest that something is badly awry, with our schools and with our boys." Of course, such crude and hurtful behavior has always been displayed by some pre-teen and teen boys. The difference is that kids used to be punished for such rudeness, and even ostracized by their peers as the "bad kids." It seems that in many cases, girls have just learned to put up with the behavior, teachers have given up, and parents don't have a clue. As for the boys themselves? Well, they don't seem to have any place to look for direction, boundaries, and what their role should be. Society doesn't teach them to be gentlemen anymore. No one tells them to open the door for girls, to offer a chair, or to even watch their language and banter around their female friends. Such acts of respect and thoughtfulness are all but gone—they were thrown out when radical feminism started demanding "equal" treatment in every aspect of the word.

Dress Your Son in Respect

Equal pay for equal work? Of course. Equal opportunity for the sexes? Absolutely. But treating our daughters like "one of the boys"? I think we've robbed both our young males and females of their dignity and pride by allowing manners to be discarded in the name of "equality."

Barney Brawer, director of the Boys' Project at Tufts University, told *Education Week*: "We've deconstructed the old version of manhood, but we've not constructed a new version." Mr. Brawer could not be more right. Radical feminism and the media have created a cultural vacuum on the topic of manhood. Respectful behavior is treated as sexist and backwards. And the sex education taught in most public schools only adds to the problem—young men are expected to have sex with our daughters but are taught the most respectful way to treat our little girls is to wear a condom.

The problem is a failure to teach our sons what it truly means to be a strong, masculine, respectful male. And, of course, if disrespectful behavior continues to increase in the teen years, it will only manifest itself more powerfully and negatively in marriage. The sons of today are the husbands and fathers of tomorrow. If we want to reclaim the family as the healthy nucleus of American society, we must reclaim our sons.

Refuse to allow modern culture to be the etiquette class for your son. Teach him that a respectful attitude and his becoming a gentleman is necessary to succeed in all facets of life. Your son must learn that respect entails protecting the women in his life, honoring a woman's chastity and name, and acting like a gentleman towards other men and his elders.

IN YOUR SHOES

My friend Amy was recently at a restaurant with her family, which included her 11-year-old brother, Lyde. Next to her family, the waiters were setting up a large table for what was clearly going to be a big group event. After about ten minutes, a group of high school-aged women and men came bounding up the stairs, laughing and chatting. After some loud shuffling and scuffling, they all found their seats and began ordering.Lyde, who had just finished a cotillion (dance) class, had been watching and closely observing how this young social group interacted. He took Amy's family by surprise when he indignantly chimed in saying, "Those boys are not very respectful!" The family slowly put down their forks, a bit caught off-guard by the remark. Lyde's mother asked, "Why do you say that?"He replied,"Well, all of the boys came in and grabbed the best seats for themselves, and then made the girls climb around them for their chairs. The boys should have waited until all the girls picked a seat, pulled out their chairs for them, and then took the leftover seats. What they did was really disrespectful to the girls." The parents sat in stunned silence.The good news about the above example is: they can be taught! It doesn't take much to open even the youngest of eyes to reality that there is honor in honoring others.

Julie, a recent college graduate, shared how young men frequently bolt in the door ahead of her, and even reported on how one slammed the door in her face, causing her to fall down. Unfortunately, those are only her mild encounters with young men who have been taught nothing of manners. She also shared about overhearing college men referring to women saying things like, "last night I smacked that a**" or making fun of women's appearance or physical flaws. When did young men start getting away with acting so disrespectful? You can pretty much trace it to the simultaneous break-down of the family, the rise of radical feminism, and the onslaught of crude media. These dynamics have created the "perfect storm" and our young men are being flung around like *garbage. Of course, if someone is treated like garbage, they have a tendency to treat others that way. While we as parents can't magically turn back the clock to a more civilized society in general, we can control what we teach about how to treat others. We have a responsibility to teach that degrading or even thoughtless behavior toward others will not happen on our watch and should never happen, even when no one is watching. We must be pro-active in teaching that thoughtfulness is next to godliness, and that considering others and their feelings is a mark of the highest character. Not all young men are rude and crass. There are plenty of kind and gracious young men with strong character out there, but they are becoming an increasingly rare find. Sadly, parents who do not teach their sons to be considerate rob them of a virtue—the loss of which will harm them the rest of their lives. They will find it harder to please their teachers and bosses, and will be less able to find the type of woman who will stand by them, admire them, and give them the respect that men so deeply crave for themselves.*

FROM MY HOME TO YOURS

■ One tool which seems to be losing popularity these days but could use a good come back is the concept of a cotillion or etiquette class for your pre-teen sons. There's just something delightful about watching them put on coats and ties and forcing them to interact with girls in a room run by adults with old-fashioned manners. If you stay and watch, you just might be reminded of a few good rules of civility yourself.

■ Look for media examples (although they are few and far between) that show the power and masculinity of men who are loyal and true. Take Mel Gibson's "The Patriot" or his epic movie, "Braveheart." (NOTE: I think these are appropriate for teenagers, but not younger boys.) In both movies Gibson was loyal and true to his family, his faith, and his belief in freedom. Although far from perfect, the characters Gibson portrayed believed in fidelity and marriage. Speak to your son frequently about the power and strong character that comes from being a person of undying commitment and absolute loyalty to someone else. You must also teach him the value of being loyal and true to an ideal that is bigger than himself—ideas like freedom, equality and standing up for the defenseless.

■ The most natural way to teach manners is at home at your own dinner table. See every meal as an opportunity to practice dining etiquette—for your sons and daughters. And, as my son Drew reminds me, the most effective thing you can tell your sons about having thoughtful behavior and good manners is, "The girls really do like it."

■ One of the finest youth organizations for sons remains the Boy Scouts. It provides parents with amazing opportunities to work with their kids and each other to raise young men of character and responsibility. It is truly a blessing to be in a room with a bunch of teenage boys and have my presence be absolutely natural—even desired. I'm so thankful that my husband and I were able to raise our two boys with the principles and handbook of the Scouts at our side.

The way Scouting is set-up is unique: parents help their sons and the boys help each other. I could tell story after story about how being involved in Scouting created a network of parents that worked hard to help their sons and the other boys in the troop succeed. Because of my husband's hard work and leadership with Scouts, my boys' commitment to seeing the program all the way through, and the dedication and support of the other parents, twelve boys in the age range of our sons went through the teen years as Scouts and every one of them became Eagles. And, even though becoming involved in scouting or even obtaining the rank of Eagle does not guarantee perfect sons (is there such a creature?), Scouting does provide an organized framework and an established code of behavior that, if practiced by all young men, would rid the world of many ills. Even the families whose boys don't stay with Scouting all the way through find the program to be a great encouragement and reinforcement of sound values. And there is another tremendous benefit: a network of families who are teaching their boys the same traditional and bedrock principles. The Boy Scout motto and law are so "on target" and timeless that I've listed them all for you:

SCOUT OATH (OR PROMISE)

On my honor I will do my best
To do my duty to God and my country
and to obey the Scout Law;
To help other people at all times;
To keep myself physically strong,
mentally awake, and morally straight.

SCOUT LAW

Trustworthy. A Scout tells the truth. He keeps his promises. Honesty is part of his code of conduct. People can depend on him.

Loyal. A Scout is true to his family, Scout leaders, friends, school, and nation.

Helpful. A Scout is concerned about other people. He does things willingly for others without pay or reward.

Friendly. A Scout is a friend to all. He is a brother to other Scouts. He seeks to understand others. He respects those with ideas and customs other than his own.

Courteous. A Scout is polite to everyone regardless of age or position. He knows good manners make it easier for people to get along together.

Kind. A Scout understands there is strength in being gentle. He treats others as he wants to be treated. He does not hurt or kill harmless things without reason.

Obedient. A Scout follows the rules of his family, school, and troop. He obeys the laws of his community and country. If he thinks these rules and laws are unfair, he tries to have them changed in an orderly manner rather than disobey them.

Cheerful. A Scout looks for the bright side of things. He cheerfully does tasks that come his way. He tries to make others happy.

Thrifty. A Scout works to pay his way and to help others. He saves for unforeseen needs. He protects and conserves natural resources. He carefully uses time and property.

Brave. A Scout can face danger even if he is afraid. He has the courage to stand for what he thinks is right even if others laugh at or threaten him.

Clean. A Scout keeps his body and mind fit and clean. He goes around with those who believe in living by these same ideals. He helps keep his home and community clean.

Reverent. A Scout is reverent toward God. He is faithful in his religious duties. He respects the beliefs of others.

Scouting also created countless wonderful memories of fun times for us with our boys that we will forever cherish. Identifying and becoming involved with an organization like the Boy Scouts is even more important for the single parent.

Of course, the best way to teach your son to be a gentleman is to model it yourself. If you've been negligent in either directly teaching your son about basic manners and respect or practicing it for him, vow to change your ways this very day.

When talking to your son about respect, begin by teaching him that the principle of respect is rooted in an understanding of the inherent dignity of other people. The Golden Rule (see "Let the Golden Rule, Rule Your Home") teaches us to treat others as we would like to be treated—a concept based in the idea that each of us is endowed with dignity by a Creator and worthy of being treated with honor.

ACT NOW

Date _____

Today I sat down with my son and talked about the lifelong value of treating others with respect. We began working through a book on manners or I enrolled him/us in an etiquette class.

_____
Signature

MORE HELP

- Dr. James Dobson of Focus on the Family has two wonderful resources on parenting boys, *Bringing Up Boys* and *Dare to Discipline*. Focus on the Family also has a website devoted to parenting and discipline tips broken down by age groups and specific topics at family.org.

- *Breakaway Magazine*, also produced by Focus on the Family, is written for older boys and young men. Buying a young man in your life a subscription to the magazine will provide him with the tools and principles necessary to become a man of honor. It is one of the few items written specifically for young men that does something other than feed on their sexual and hormonal vulnerabilities.

- There are also a few great books on manners for you to use with your son. The very best method to use such books is to read them with your son. When doing so, make sure your son realizes that learning manners and respect should not be seen as a burden, but rather as something that will set him apart from his peers and help him to succeed in school, dating, and his career. Respect given is respect earned.

- My favorite books on manners for men and boys are John Bridges' *How to be a Gentleman: A Timely Guide to Timely Manners* and *50 Things Every Young Gentleman Should Know*.

- Emily Post's *Etiquette*, her revised book on manners, is also a classic with simple and digestible sections. The website for the Emily Post Institute, emilypost.com, is full of excellent resources for parents and children of all ages on a wide range of topics such as etiquette in the workplace for teens.

Obtain A Reliable Internet Filter

THE CHALLENGE

According to a study by the London School of Economics, nine out of ten children who go online (by the way, many of them just doing their homework) will view pornography. A 2006 study by the Kaiser Family Foundation shows that seven out of ten view the porn unintentionally—at least the first time. In other words, even when kids are acting responsibly and innocently, the pornographers are so fixated on creating new porn addicts that they have made it virtually impossible for children to escape their grasp. Think about it—90 percent of all kids on the internet will be subjected to the sexual images and values of the perverted pornographers that are rampant in the e-world. And, tragically, according to a 2006 report by the National Center for

Missing and Exploited Children, one out of three children who view pornography are doing it intentionally.

Our culture has become so obsessed with "sexualized everything" that our children's innocence is all but gone. I believe there should be a protected space in childhood where kids don't have sex forced upon them—physically or mentally. And, for crying out loud, if you as a mom or dad aren't building that space in your own home, how on earth can we expect them to have it anyplace else? Let me be clear: If your kids consume hard-core pornography in your home via the internet, you are the one to blame. The fantastic news is that this is one problem you can easily fix.

Mere exposure to pornography inflicts a great deal of damage to developing attitudes, psyches, and morality. Jill Manning, a former visiting fellow at The Heritage Foundation, outlined the personal cost of pornography to children in a paper she presented to a special U.S. Senate subcommittee. Her analysis of the peer-reviewed research reveals that pornography consumption by children is associated with the following trends (just to name a few):

- Developing tolerance toward sexually explicit material, thereby requiring more novel or bizarre material to achieve the same level of arousal or interest.
- Overestimating the prevalence of less common harmful, sexual practices (such as group sex, bestiality, and sadomasochistic activity.)
- Abandoning the goal of sexual activity with exclusivity to one partner
- Perceiving promiscuity as a normal state of interaction.
- Developing cynical attitudes about love.
- Believing that raising children and having a family is an unattractive prospect.

■ Developing a negative body image, especially for girls.

The solution to this problem is easy: Get a reliable internet filter, and get it now.

FROM MY HOME TO YOURS

Despite the fact that our kids are being body-slammed by pornography, only four out of ten parents of children age nine or older have installed parental controls on their computers, reports a survey by the Kaiser Family Foundation. (And what about for the kids under nine? Heaven only knows. The survey only gave results for the older children—yet, younger and younger children are routinely online in many homes.) Yet, a report by the Pew Internet and American Life Project revealed that 62 percent of parents fear that kids are seeing and reading inappropriate content. Can you see the disconnect here? Even while some sixty percent of parents understand that they should be worried about their kid's exposure to harmful material, only forty percent have bothered to do anything about it. And there's another 40 percent of parents that don't seem to have a clue that every time their precious child surfs the net, the likelihood is that graphic sex images await them. Which percentage are you in?

There are now several reliable, inexpensive filters you can download in minutes onto your computer. You can find them at Focus on the Family (family.org), the American Family Association (afa.net), and Web Wise Kids (webwisekids.org). I've researched many filters and one of my favorites is available from bsafe.com. It takes only a few minutes and a few keystrokes to download the filter directly onto your computer. The cost is about 50 bucks a year, and the system is updated constantly so it stays ahead of the porn industry's attempts to out-smart filtering systems. The BSafe filter is also password protected so you can override the system if it blocks a site by mistake. You also receive a weekly report via e-mail letting you know what sites users in your home attempted to visit—a very useful tool when you have guests in your home. I've used the filter for a long time, so my kids know about the tracking system. However, the week that two brothers were visiting us from out-of-town, my report revealed that someone had attempted to visit six hard-core porn sites. Thank the Good Lord, their attempts were blocked. Had I not taken the time to secure the internet for those in my care, these two young boys would have consumed hard-core pornography in my own home and possibly exposed my own children while the rest of us slept peacefully just down the hallway. Think about it: we go to great lengths as parents to secure our doors and windows at night—yet, for far too many parents the open portal of the internet allows every kind of perversion to enter our homes—and to attack the innocence and sensibilities of our kids.

Some parents who want to protect their kids online may have concerns that a filter would block health and reproductive information that might actually help their sons and daughters understand more about their ever-changing bodies. Good news on this front: there is no need for concern. FamilyFacts.org summarizes a study on blocking software that was detailed in the article, "Does Pornography-Blocking Software Block Access to Health Information on the Internet?" As published in the *Journal of the American Medical Association* in 2002. The summary reads, "Pornography-blocking software has minimal impact on one's access to information about sexual and reproductive health. For example, filtering software set at moderate settings blocks only 5 percent of health information while blocking 90 percent of pornographic content online." The filters I recommend also contain password protective override systems in case you, as a parent, believe a safe site has been mistakenly blocked. With a simple password and verification from you, the site becomes accessible. So what are you waiting for?

IN YOUR SHOES

After giving a lecture about my book *Home Invasion* at The Heritage Foundation, a mother of five with whom I have been friends for fifteen years approached me with distress etched across her face, "Can I meet with you privately for a few minutes? I feel so convicted about something." My friend has been heavily involved in the battle for decency in our culture for many years as have I. Yet, as is the case with most parents, she is technically challenged. She spoke with tears in her eyes as she shared an all-too-familiar horror story:

"I've known that I need a filter on our internet. But my husband and I always seem to be having computer problems and we just feel overwhelmed by all the technology. I thought I could keep my kids safe by monitoring their usage myself. But several weeks ago our eight-year-old daughter awoke us in the middle of the night crying her heart out. We thought she was sick. Our precious little girl then said between sobs, 'I've done something very bad. I was on the computer and saw some very bad pictures.'" The mother then tried to assure her daughter that it wasn't her fault that she had stumbled across the photos—that she shouldn't feel guilty or like a 'bad girl.' The daughter responded between breaths, "But mommy, I stayed and looked for a very long time." What a tragedy. An innocent eight-year-old girl from a responsible, conscientious family had vivid sex acts etched in her brain even before she knew what sex was. The child had been suffering for days with her own torment and guilt, replaying over and over in her mind the horrible scenes that she didn't understand, but that she instinctively knew were wrong. And it all could have

been avoided with the simple ten minute act of downloading a filter.

OTHER ONLINE SAFETY TIPS:

❑ Never allow your children to have internet connections in their bedrooms. Put the internet in a common room so that everyone in the family is accountable for how they are spending their time online. One reader of my Townhall column, Julia, suggested a great tip: *"We have an older, slower computer in our sixteen-year-old son's room, but no internet connection. He can write papers and make spreadsheets, and that's about all! He has to bring his disk down to the "big computer" to print out his work.'"*

❑ Set limits on internet usage. The problem is not just with content, it is with the hours and hours many kids spent online when they should be in face-to-face interactions with family and friends.

❑ Talk to your child about safety on the World Wide Web. Teach them how to navigate the web safely and to recognize areas of danger (more on this in the next chapter, "Keep Your Kids Safe In Online Social Networking"). WebWiseKids.com offers a great interactive game that teaches your children life-saving tips for using the net.

❑ Make it a rule that children never give out family or personal contact information on the web.

❑ Never share passwords to sites, even with a friend. But insist that your child provides you with their passwords for MySpace, FaceBook and any other sites they use. Your mantra should be, "I'm paying for the computer, the room, the electricity, the internet connection, and everything else you see. No password—no access." Let them know you will be checking their sites often in order to keep them safe. There is no room for compromise here, and you should never, ever let the "world" or your own "friends" tell you otherwise.

❑ Have rules for which games your children can download or buy. Understand that many of these games are violent, sexual, or just plain time-wasters. For the games you do allow them to play, make time to play with them on occasion.

❑ Remind your children that not everything they read online is accurate. Encourage them to double-check facts across multiple sites and against trusted sources

❑ Explain the concept of "intellectual property" and "plagiarism." Let your kids know it is stealing to use someone else's music, art, or words without either purchasing them or crediting them.

ACT NOW

Date _____

Download an internet filter from BSafe or other reliable service right now. Go to your computer, and do it.

❑ I secured a filter for my computer on _____(date).

_____
Signature

MORE HELP

- WebWiseKids.org has a lot of great tools to teach internet safety for both parents and kids. I'm very proud to serve as a volunteer on the Advisory Committee for WebWiseKids, and to recommend a great parental resource tool, Wired With Wisdom®, which, "has been specifically designed to be a user-friendly solution for parents. In addition, police officers and other professionals have recognized the value of the program and have utilized it to obtain valuable vocational safety training." Wired With Wisdom® is available online or as a download and features five learning components, each of which can be completed in only 20 minutes. The issues addressed include:

  - Social Networking
  - Personal Websites
  - The World Wide Web
  - Chatrooms
  - Instant Messaging
  - E-Mail
  - Cell phone dangers
  - Emerging technology

- I also serve as a volunteer on the Internet Safety Council for "Enough is Enough!" (enough.org), an organization which I was very proud to help found way back in 1992. Even before the internet era, it was obvious to me that illegal and child pornography were making victims and addicts of many people. My dear friends Dee Jepsen, Becky Norton Dunlop, Sarah Blankenship and others worked very hard with the National Coalition Against Pornography to inform women of the dangers of pornography on our lives, safety, self-esteem, and culture. Today, the organization is run by Donna Rice Hughes and has refocused their ef-

continued

Obtain a Reliable Internet Filter

forts on the keeping kids safe from online dangers. No one has done a better job at compiling resources for parents to use in keeping their kids safe online than Donna. No one. Enough is Enough's many invaluable tools includes the Internet Safety 101: Empowering Parents Program video and work book. The CD and book contain list after list of gadgets you can use to protect your kids online, on their cell phones, and on their iPhones. They also provide facts, testimonials, age-based guidelines, and simple to understand explanations of all the latest technologies and even a look at what is to come. EIE also maintains two great sites: In their words, "Enough.org and Protectkids.com...serve as a clearinghouse for Internet safety and victim assistance resources. Their purpose is to educate the public about the dangers of Internet pornography and sexual predators as it relates to children and families. In addition, the websites are designed to promote and provide prevention awareness and empower parents and other adult child-caregivers to implement safety measures including the Rules 'N' Tools[SM] needed to protect children from online dangers."

Keep Your Kids Safe In Online Social Networking

THE CHALLENGE

There's no question that the Internet has proved to be a huge blessing. A world of information can be found at our fingertips; more moms and dads get to work in their homes instead of spending so much time in the office; we can access the world and many of its wonders with the simple click of a mouse, and explore new cultures without leaving our living rooms. The rise of social networking sites such as Facebook, MySpace, and many others allow people of all ages to easily stay in touch with family and friends—and to make new acquaintances.

For the most part, such contact—which typically occurs in e-mail, Internet "chat rooms" (virtual rooms where people "sit around and talk") and other online forums—is harmless. But, parents beware: like any public playground or theme park, chat rooms are also places where pedophiles and other perverts like to prowl.

It seems nearly every week there's a news story about some sick individual who has preyed on children and teens via the internet. While we often think the youngest of children are at the greatest risk, the fact is that the average age for child abduction is twelve years old. Why? This is the age when our kids are more independent and are first learning to protect themselves. The sad truth is also that our teens are increasingly vulnerable to victimization because they are spending more and more time online talking with strangers, and parents seem to be unaware of the fact that evil adults often anonymously search the internet and quietly spy on chat room conversations in search of prey. Chat rooms and sites such as MySpace.com have become playgrounds for sexual predators, luring kids into situations of abuse and even death. The problem is so extensive that there have even been a plethora of television shows like "America's Most Wanted" that feature sting operations and horror stories of adults meeting kids to have sex with them. According to the National Center for Missing and Exploited Children, two out of every five missing children ages 15 to 17 are abducted in connection with Internet activity.

The online dangers aren't confined to the chat rooms, unfortunately: parents who have found porn in their e-mail inboxes, been tormented by raunchy pop-up images, or have unwittingly, and way too easily, stumbled across a porn site, must realize that any kid who spends time on the Internet will not only be victimized by such images, but will, due to natural childhood curiosity, be drawn into them.

The internet is a place for perverts to "shop" for children without detection. These perverts have cunningly studied how to present themselves as "friends" to your kids. They often pretend to be teenagers and know just how to pry and push into the emotional turmoil that marks the teen years. Recent polling of teens shows that over 50 percent of kids who enter chat rooms—where the conversation can all too often turn raunchy and racy—say they have given out personal information to complete strangers including their phone numbers, home addresses, and where they go to school.

And the risks associated with "random" innocent Internet surfing are all too real. Statistics reveal, for example, that children as young as five are now regularly being exposed to porn online. Online pornography is more than a $10 billion a year industry, working 24/7 to make porn addicts out of our kids—and too often succeeding. It's a devastating problem that destroys the innocence of our children and threatens their emotional, moral, social, and spiritual development.

Here are a few alarming facts every parent should know (all of which can be found and referenced on the Web Wise Kids website (webwisekids.org):

- 96% of students ages 9 to 17 who have access to the Internet have used social networking technologies.
- 71% of students ages 9 to 17 use social networking sites on a weekly basis.
- 64% of teens post photos or videos of themselves online; 58% post information about where they live. Females are far more likely than male teens to post personal photos or videos of themselves.
- Nearly one in 10 teens (8%) has posted his or her cell phone number online.
- 58% of teens don't think posting photos or other personal info on social networking sites is unsafe.
- 32% of all teens and 43% of teens active in social networking have been contacted online by a complete stranger.

- Boys are more likely than girls to post personal information.
- Among teens active in social networking sites, 61% post the name of their city or town, 49% post their school's name, 29% post their email address, and 29% post their last name.
- 69% of teens regularly receive personal messages online from people they don't know and most of them don't tell a trusted adult about it.
- 23% of children have had an encounter with a stranger on the Internet, including 7% of children who reported having met someone in the real world from the Internet.
- 79% of sexual solicitation incidents happened to youth while they were using their home computer.
- 40% of solicitations began with a solicitor communicating with a youth through an instant message, or IM.
- 56% of solicitations contained a request for the youth to send photographs of themselves to the solicitor and 27% of solicitations contained a request for the youth to send a sexual picture of themselves.

Another problem for kids who go online is "cyberbullying." The World Wide Web has taken old-fashioned playground taunts to a new and disturbing level. Bullies can reach a much wider audience now, at all hours of the day, tormenting kids who have been socially ostracized. The group Internet Solutions for Kids says that as many as 34 percent of children have been bullied online, and around 16 percent say they're targeted regularly. Web Wise Kids says that cyberbullying is most prevalent among 15- and 16-year-olds, particularly among girls.

In many ways, the new cyberbullying is worse than the "in person" kind. The Internet seems more like a "virtual world," not only to kids, but to adults—a place where some people say and do cruel things they might never say or do in person. That's the focus, in fact, of a series of ads launched in 2008 by the Ad Council. The ads feature a young girl who suddenly starts saying horrible things about a classmate, right in front of a group of shocked students that include the girl she's targeting. "If you wouldn't say it in person," the narrator asks, "why say it online?" The words "delete cyberbullying" are then typed onto the screen—and erased.

You are the protector: it's up to you to leave your techno-comfort zone and learn about this "brave new world." We must teach our children that the time-honored advice of "don't talk to strangers" applies to the internet, too.

A great way to get started is to order the computer game, *Missing*. Web Wise Kids has used it in hundreds of schools to teach adults and kids how to be safe online. It's easy to use, and is endorsed by The Salvation Army, Boys and Girls Clubs, many public and private schools, and the Los Angeles Police Department, just to name a few. In the game, kids must attempt to rescue a teen who has been enticed to live "the good life" with an adult he meets online. The situation is extremely realistic, because it's modeled on the techniques of perverts who stalk kids in the real world. Kids learn to recognize dangerous patterns of online conversations and what to do if they find themselves in such a situation.

One of the game's biggest fans is Katie, who at fifteen-years-old nearly fell victim to a twenty-two-year-old she met online. Because Katie had played *Missing* when she was a pre-teen, she recognized the e-mail pattern of the man she had begun to fall "in love" with as a predator, and told her parents of her fears. Her folks contacted law enforcement and handed over all the computer records of the conversations. Sure enough, Katie's "boyfriend" turned out to be the primary suspect in the rape of a thirteen-year-old girl. With Katie's testimony about his method of seduction, which matched the testimony of his rape victim, he was sentenced to twenty years in prison, and Katie avoided falling victim to the worst of crimes.

❏ **Set clear rules about computer usage.** Explain how much non-school time your child can spend on the computer, and when he can do so—after his schoolwork is completed, for example.

❏ **Make sure any computers are located in a family area.** Some 25 percent of teens say their parents know "little" or "nothing" about what they do online. This is a problem primarily for parents who make the mistake of letting a child have a computer in his room. Our computers are located in an open room so they can be easily monitored. It's a very bad idea to put TVs or computers in kids' bedrooms. You never know who or what they might come across or how much time they might spend blankly staring at the screen.

❏ **Install an Internet filter.** I cannot stress this enough. According to Pew Research, 54 percent of parents with teenagers use Internet filters—a big jump from 2000. But that's not nearly enough. No parent should allow his child to use a computer without an Internet filter; the potential for trouble is simply too great.

The best solution should be the most obvious: talk to your kids about using the Internet responsibly! Only about 41 percent of teens report that their parents talk to them "a lot" about Internet safety—that leaves nearly six out of ten who aren't doing their job. The web is a window to the world for your kids—but it is also a window into their world for others. Be sure they know that they should come to you immediately if anybody online begins asking personal questions or attempting to invade their privacy. Make them understand that it's better to be "overcautious" than sorry.

Mom, Dad, you should be the ultimate "filter." It's your responsibility to watch for garbage that might slip through, to warn your kids about online predators, and to teach them not to talk to strangers online. When you fail to take such action, it's as if you have given the perverts your permission to stalk your sons and daughters.

IN YOUR SHOES

For some reason we as parents still think that our own kids aren't really at risk. We develop a false sense of security if we live in safe neighborhoods. But because the internet knows no geographic boundaries, even families in the smallest of towns and best neighborhoods are at risk to predators from the worst parts of town, and indeed, all over the world. I grew up in a charming, relaxed southern town of Lakeland, Florida. I was dismayed to see the following story in my hometown newspaper:

The Lakeland Ledger, Sept. 30, 2008—A Lakeland man was arrested Tuesday after deputies say he picked up a fifteen-year-old girl he met on MySpace.

Joseph Christopher Kern, twenty-three, was charged with using a computer or Internet to solicit a child for a sexual act, a third-degree felony, and traveling to meet a minor for sexual activity and lewd molestation, second-degree felonies.

According to the report, Kern had several sexual conversations with the Lakeland girl on the Web site MySpace.com on Monday and Tuesday. During the online conversations, Kern told the girl to change her age on the Web site to eighteen so he could avoid 'trouble' and asked her for a mature relationship, the report said. The girl indicated in one message that she wanted to wait before any sexual activity and Kern indicated he would try to wait.

About 8 p.m. Monday, Kyle Stinson, twenty-one, drove Kern to meet the girl and one of her friends, deputies said. They took the two to Stinson's home, where the report said Kern and the girl engaged in sexual activity.

The girl returned home about 1 a.m., after her mother had called her demanding that she come home, the report said.

Both Stinson and Kern were charged with interfering with child custody, a third-degree felony.

ACT NOW

Date _____

Today I started making my home a safe place for my children to go online. I pledge to continuously update myself about Internet dangers, and to ensure that my children understand how to use the Internet safely.

_____

Signature

MORE HELP

There are many excellent organizations and Web sites to help parents "Web-proof" their home (which also illustrates how wide and serious the problem of online dangers really is). I mention several of these sites in "Obtain a Reliable Internet Filter," but another particularly good one is Internet Solutions for Kids (is4k.com).

You should also check out komando.com, the site of Kim Komando, a web-savvy mother who hosts a weekly three-hour call-in talk radio show. Her "10 Commandments for Kids Online" is something you may want to print out and post in your home.

I already mentioned the *Internet Safety 101: Empower Parents* workbook and DVD in the last chapter, but I really cannot emphasize this set of materials enough. Ordering and using it will make you the technology master in your home, and will equip you to protect your children in ways you didn't even know you needed to! You can use the DVD or workbook alone or together, and they are divided into useful sections that you can use one at a time. The materials teach you about the prevalence, dangers, and harms of pornography usage by kids; what fuels and how to avoid online predators; the basic tools you need to keep your kids safe; and lists of great resources. Internet Safety 101 is designed for both individual and group use, and can be ordered for around $ 30.00 through enough.org or by calling 888-744-0004.

Let The Golden Rule, Rule Your Home

THE CHALLENGE

It's simple: "Do unto others as you would have them do unto you." This biblical wisdom is so self-evident that it is universally admired, even by those who profess no faith in God at all. Yet how constantly we fail to fulfill this ideal.

It's truly the basic tenant for human relations. Imagine the pain the world would be free of if only everyone followed the Golden Rule. Imagine the good that could be accomplished, the human suffering that would be replaced with human achievement if we each treated others the way we want to be treated. But, fat chance, right? I mean, how many of us practice it in our own homes with the people that we are supposed to love the most? With divorced and broken families now the norm in American society, who is modeling the Golden Rule for our children?

The solution is obvious but the practice is hard: begin putting others first. And that includes taking the time and energy to teach your teens and kids to do the same.

Part and parcel of this responsibility means teaching good manners. I don't just mean learning which fork to use at a formal dinner, but enforcing basic consideration for others. That kind of consideration, of looking out for others, doesn't come naturally. It has to be taught by giving our children something good to emulate.

There's a strong correlation between active parenting and teaching the civility and thoughtfulness that make the world go 'round. How else would children learn to avoid quarreling and whining? Where would they learn to offer someone a seat if the bus is full? How would they learn to take pride in their chores? How would they learn to say "please," "thank you," and "you're welcome"? God doesn't put us on Earth knowing these things.

Children learn when parents take the time to teach them and to enforce family standards. Part-time parenting that says, "Go to your room, watch television, get on the computer, amuse yourself because I have neither the time nor the inclination to make you do otherwise," produces children who will, in turn, think of themselves before the needs of even their closest loved ones.

In the competitiveness of the modern culture, it's easy to lose sight of that. As author Dr. V. Gilbert Beers says, "What our children become is infinitely more important than what our children will do."

In other words, it's who they are becoming on the inside that matters most.

The greatest gift we can impart to our children is to teach them to love God with all of their hearts and minds—and to love their neighbors as they love themselves. The toxicity of our culture makes it more important than ever for parents to take an active role in developing the character traits that enable our sons and daughters to live their lives in a manner that strengthens and reveals this call to love.

It's an uphill battle, to be sure. In *Something for Nothing: The All-Consuming Desire that Turns the American Dream into a Social Nightmare*, self-help author Brian Tracy describes how mankind's inborn nature to be "lazy, greedy, ambitious, selfish, vain, ignorant, and impatient" without regard to others, has plunged our nation into crisis.

Of course, the propensity of humans to scheme about how to get something for nothing is certainly not new to the human condition or to Americans. And the devastating effects that such expectations and attitudes have on the individual and his personal character have been well documented throughout history. As Thomas Jefferson once said, "The worst day of a man's life is when he sits down and begins thinking about how he can get something for nothing."

A huge challenge of parenthood is trying to shape our children into young gentlemen and ladies who will spend their lives with a propensity to give and earn, rather than to merely receive and take.

As Brian Tracy points out, the best efforts of even the most loving and committed parents to raise children of character are often thwarted because we have failed to realize the necessity of channeling children's natural drives into positive behaviors. This is especially difficult when all around us our society rewards and encourages the "me first with no concern for others" attitude that harms both individuals and civil society.

Commit to model the Golden Rule and teach your kids how to do the same. We can't simply blame society and throw up our hands, however tempting that may seem at times. Parents may not be able to control the overall culture (although we certainly should influence it to the best of our ability), but we have the responsibility and privilege to determine the lessons taught within our own homes.

FROM MY HOME TO YOURS

Here are five easy ways to begin living and teaching the Golden Rule in your home:

1) **Invest time in your kids.** Teaching the Golden Rule starts with investing more time in their lives. As Brian Tracy reminds us:

   Many parents want to get something for nothing in child rearing. They want to be seen as excellent parents without paying the price that this requires. How does a child spell "love"? Answer: "T-I-M-E!" Something for nothing parents try to get by on the cheap, spending their precious and irreplaceable time in all the wrong places. The solution to the problems of marriage and parenting is simple. Spend more time with the people you care about the most.

Even the busiest parents can make a concerted effort to be around their children. If you want to shape their values, there's no substitute for simply being there.

2) **Be a role model**. Your children will emulate you—so be a good example! I can practically guarantee that if you find a child that is kind and considerate of others, that child has parents who exhibit the same characteristics. If we want children who are patient, for example, we need to *be* patient—not only with them, but when we feel exasperated about something (especially in their presence). The same goes for other character traits. Let them see you exercising self-control, *not* interrupting (even them), being honest, doing good work, and putting others first. You can be sure it will rub off.

Let the Golden Rule, Rule Your Home

3) **Share stories of kindness**. One effective way to teach principles to your kids is to share stories of how lives are impacted by the deeds of others. Pick up movies that impart good morals—ones that show good triumphing over evil, that don't mock authority figures, or show the "good guys" engaging in boorish or immoral behavior. Many seemingly "family friendly" books and shows actually teach some bad lessons. Choose carefully what your family reads and watches, and start colleting a library of both books and videos that teach decency and thoughtfulness.

4) **Practice generosity in front of your kids.** Ours is a selfish culture. You and your family may not be rich, but you can be generous. One of the simple things I do is carry snacks or inspirational reading materials in my car that can be given to others. Since we live near a big city, we often see homeless people on the street. Sometimes they walk by our car holding a sign asking for money. While most people look the other way and pretend they aren't there, several years ago I made it a policy to acknowledge them as human beings in need of love and comfort. Regardless of how they got there, I try to remember that if it were my kid that was homeless for any reason—even his own doing—I would pray for God to send someone—anyone—to be kind and generous to him. I decided that whenever possible, I would answer that prayer of some distant mother I will never know, and be that person for her grown child. This doesn't mean I always give them money, but I do give them something. Sometimes it is a book I believe in, sometimes it is an apple, sometimes it is a profession of faith. I especially do this when my kids are with me, because more than just about anything in the world, I want them to grow up to be generous and to genuinely love their fellow man.

5) **"Practice Random Acts of Kindness."** I'm not sure who first came up with that phrase, but it is what we should do every day—starting with our own families! Encourage your teens to do simple, kind things for each other—like pitching in and cleaning each other's rooms, remembering to invite their sibling along when going to Starbucks, or just taking the time to talk to each other. Encourage them to offer to cut the neighbor's grass, or simply pick up the newspaper off the sidewalk and put it on their doorstep. Sometimes when my kids are grumpy or whining, I say, "Think of something nice to do for someone else right now—and go do it." Teaching our children to take the focus off of themselves and put that energy into helping others shows them that no matter how bad things are, they can always make life better for someone else.

It also shows them just how many blessings they have.

IN YOUR SHOES

Sometimes, a seemingly casual remark—the kind that arises naturally out of time spent together—can make a big impact in a child's life and truly affect his moral outlook and behavior. Consider this story from Dr. Robert Shaw, author of *The Epidemic: The Rot of American Culture, Absentee and Permissive Parenting, and the Resultant Plague of Joyless, Selfish Children*:

A significant memory from my childhood is of a conversation I had with my father about a friend's family. My father would come home from work early, and we would both head

Let the Golden Rule, Rule Your Home

for the den, where we played checkers and talked. It was during World War II, and everyone knew there were people engaging in black market activities. I remember telling my dad about my friend Joey, whose family seemed to be getting richer by the day. They had a new Cadillac, went on impressive vacations, and bought lots of expensive toys. Of course, I was envious, but what I remember most is my father's response: "I wouldn't do that. I prefer to sleep well at night." And I knew exactly what he meant—he wouldn't do anything that would give him a guilty conscience or interfere with his sense of well-being. I saw that my father stood for something. That phrase became a shorthand reminder throughout my life that I, too, wanted to "sleep well."

ACT NOW

Date _____

Today I began letting the Golden Rule, rule my home. I pledge to help my children understand that the two greatest commandments are to love God and love other people, and to model these for them.

_____
Signature

MORE HELP

- *Everyday Graces*—Karen Santorum has produced a full guidebook of the manners children should know. She covers the bases—good manners at home and school, what to say and not say, how to act at the dinner table, how to wash and dress, caring for the elderly, sick, and disabled, getting along with others, good sportsmanship, what to do at church, weddings, and funerals, handling thank-you notes, and how to respect our country. It's common-sense stuff, and other books include this information. But Santorum uses stories one can't forget to illustrate her points and to show that it's not the rules, but the underlying principles that matter. It's being thoughtful. It's being helpful, generous,spectful.

- *Something for Nothing: The All-Consuming Desire that Turns the American Dream into a Social Nightmare*—Long a champion of individual freedom, personal liberty and personal responsibility, Brian Tracy is a well-sought-after speaker and consultant, having served some 1,000 corporations worldwide. He addresses a quarter of a million people each year in more than 40 countries, and has spent a lifetime observing, analyzing, and studying the human situation. He has used his experience to create an invaluable 245-page primer on psychology, economics, sociology.

- The *Family Bible Library* is a series authored by Dr. Gilbert Beers and is specifically built on what he calls "the 36 building blocks of character," such as faith, self-control, sympathy, and courage. "The traits are presented in a systematic program that enables parents to teach—and their children to learn—these crucial aspects of proper living." The series is designed to be read with your family in blocks of 15-20 minutes a day. This useful life manual will be one of your greatest practical resources for teaching your kids how to treat their fellow man. To find out more, visit the publisher's website swfamily.com.

Help Your Children To Connect Ownership Of Material Things And Privileges With Work

THE CHALLENGE

We live in a culture that is all about "me, me, me." Take a stroll through the mall on any given day and you will see children whining when they can't have the latest toy or video game, while discouraged parents shrug their shoulders and give in. Hang around any retail store and it may seem like the "Give me" generation is running the show. You hear an "I want this" and the register replies with a hearty "ching."

Overindulging children instead of teaching them the value of *earning* what they receive is a big problem. It creates an unrealistic perception of life. Eventually our children will be adults—they will have to take care of themselves as well as their future families. If they don't learn the meaning of earning through practical and real experience as children, adulthood will hit them like a slap in the face. They will feel thrown into the proverbial pool, and might not be able to swim. Childhood, while a time of great joy and innocence, is also a time to plunk children in the shallow end, with supervision and devices to help them float, and teach them how to swim with small strokes. That way, when they get to the "deep end" of adulthood, they are strong swimmers, and able to handle turbulent waters or whatever might float their way in life.

Helping children learn the value of earning provides real life skills and gives them a deep sense of satisfaction. As humans, we are natural worker bees! We love to see the fruits of our labors, whether that is a life accomplishment like building a company or everyday tasks like finishing folding a load of laundry or baking an apple pie. We are not created to lie around slothfully. Working towards a goal and feeling pride in our efforts is what drives human action. Children who learn the value of hard work and the satisfaction that comes with completing that work and earning its reward, will have a deeper sense of self-worth and capability than children who are merely given the things they desire.

However, we, as parents, should not necessarily look at desire as a bad thing. Our task is to teach our children the link between the desire to have privileges and possessions with a good work ethic.

In 2006, *Time Magazine* voted "You" as its "Person of the Year." Narcissism is deeply embedded in today's culture, and it's creeping into our children's mentality like a poison. Young people spend hours updating their MySpace page and their Facebook pages, and posting countless pictures of themselves in a million different poses.

Where are today's children learning narcissism?

For starters, they may be learning greed and laziness from our own federal spending practices. We are indeed an entitlement society, spending approximately $1,447 billion a year—around 53 percent of all annual federal expenditures—on entitlement programs like Social Security, Medicaid, and Medicare, according to studies by The Heritage Foundation. It's not surprising if our children look at society and expect someone to take care of them if they don't take care of themselves.

Why is entitlement spending relevant, you might ask? Because children who grow up in a home with an attitude of "give me," disconnected from hard work will only expand that attitude into the public sphere. A child raised with no work ethic will become an adult consumer of the entitlement culture. And study after study on child development is only proving that those children will be low-performing and unhappy adults.

Psychotherapist and author on child development, Dr. Eileen Gallo, reports on an eye-opening Harvard study about just how critical work ethic is in a child's life. She writes:

> In a 1981 article in the *American Journal of Psychiatry*, George Valliant, the director of the Study, reported that the single biggest predictor of adult mental health was "the capacity to work learned in childhood"—In other words, the development of a work ethic. Men who Valliant described as "competent and industrious at age 14"—Men who had developed a work ethic during the Industry Stage of development—were twice as likely to have warm relationships (both family and friendships), five times more likely to have well paying jobs and 16 times less likely to have suffered significant unemployment.

Christine Conners in an article for *Family Housekeeping* reports that "Sociologists Scott Coltrane and Michele Adams found that school-aged children who do chores with their fathers get along better with peers and have more friends. They also found that they are less likely to disobey teachers, cause trouble at school and are happier and more outgoing."

In other words, there is a direct, positively correlative relationship between combating an attitude of entitlement in your child's youth and his or her success later in life.

Dealing with attitudes of entitlement is easy. Identify privileges and material goods your child values, and link them to some sort of quantifiable task. You can start the next time your child asks for something.

Find ways to teach them about entrepreneurship when they are young—whether it's opening their own lemonade stand, lining up baby sitting jobs, or taking on a paper route—these time honored "classic" kids' jobs still teach great skills and give children a sense of accomplishment when done well.

One enterprising mother I know truly understands the importance of teaching the next generation about the "value of a dollar" and how critical it is to learn business skills early in life. Linda Raasch started long ago by helping her own four kids open a pretty sophisticated lemonade stand. As Linda says on her website, BIZKIDZ.com, "This venture helped teach valuable lessons about communicating with customers, promoting merchandise, and basic financial accounting. It wasn't long before all four children had learned that there was a correlation between effort and reward." Enjoying the pleasure of her own kids success, Linda decided to start a company that allows tweens and teens to open their own "online store" and become entrepreneurs at a tender age. Lora, a twelve-year-old (and among the thousands of kids who have signed up so far), says, "After having my store on BIZKIDZ.COM, I have learned that a dollar is very precious and I have learned that not everyone likes what you like so you must change your merchandise in the store often. I have also learned a lot about marketing and advertising. My mom is very involved with me. She thinks it is a great way to learn about running a business."

We all know how much fun it was to earn our first dollars as children. But if no one is there to guide and encourage us to earn honestly, spend wisely, and give to others freely, the culture of "gimmie, gim-mie" soon takes over. But it doesn't it have to be this way.

IN YOUR SHOES

Two young girls each wanted an American Girl Doll.

Amy wanted Samantha, because she liked her big brown curls and her stylish early 20th-century clothes. Karina wanted Felicity for her cute hats and puffy dresses. Both girls asked their mothers in 4th grade if they could have the doll they picked out.

Amy's parents, though they could have easily afforded to buy her every doll, told her they would need to think through a way that she could earn the doll. After a few days, they sat her down and told her that she had been a very good girl, with a good attitude, always completing her chores and homework. She had earned the right to earn the doll of her choice.

They told her that if she could memorize and recite every state capital city in the country, Samantha would be hers. They were very clear that a doll like Samantha was expensive and a very special treat, one that does not come without some work. Interestingly, each American Girl Doll has a correlating set of books and stories telling her story. In Samantha's story, she, too, asks her Grandmother for a beautiful doll. Samantha's grandmother tells her that if she dutifully does her piano lessons, she could earn the doll.

So Amy, feeling just like Samantha, eagerly memorized her state capitals. On the day she recited them, her parents bought her the doll. Amy treasured the doll, took excellent care of her, and felt deeply appreciative of the opportunity to have her.

Karina, on the other hand, asked her mother for Felicity. Her mother immediately bought her the doll. Karina had to do absolutely nothing to earn the doll. After a few weeks, she got bored with Felicity. So she asked her mother for Molly, another doll. At first her mother resisted, and suggested they just buy some more accessories for Felicity, but Karina persisted and her mother caved. A year later, Karina had every single doll. And she was still not satisfied.

Karina did not have to lift a finger to get five very expensive toys. Amy, on the other hand, spent countless hours laboring for one, and never felt a moment's yearning for anything more than what she had earned. Not only that, but she learned something valuable along the way!

Such is the way with children and possessions. And such is the way with adults and satisfaction. Humans are hard to satisfy. But we feel much more satisfied when we know that we have earned what we have.

Teaching your child that profound sense of satisfaction is a lesson that cannot be learned too early in life.

There are a few keys to teaching the lesson of the value of earning, however.

- You must be consistent and true to your word. When you promise your child something if he or she fulfills the assigned task, you must follow through. I cannot emphasize that enough! Being true to your word is key to earning your child's trust and establishing a regular pattern of work followed by just reward. Amy's parents bought her the promised doll on the day she completed the task. As adults, we know that we do not always feel the immediate fruits of our labors. But children have a short attention span, and it is very important to make the connection between work and reward as clear as possible.

- When possible, thematically link the task you give your child to the reward he or she seeks. For example, if your daughter asks for a prom dress that costs $100, tell her she can earn it by working 10 hours of community service at a center that helps underprivileged women, women who will likely never wear a prom dress. Not only will she 1) gain some perspective and realize what a true privilege it is to dress up in expensive clothes with friends and have fun, but she will 2) attach a value to something she would have otherwise taken for granted. The dress becomes a reward for her fulfilling meaningful work. I guarantee you the girl who volunteers with underprivileged women to earn her shiny new dress is far less likely to take for granted the privilege of wearing it than her friends who are bought one with no effort.

- Finally, make the task straightforward and quantifiable, something with a clear beginning and a concrete conclusion. One young woman I know had to memorize 100 Bible verses before being able to get her driver's license. Both of my own sons had to earn the rank of Eagle Scout before acquiring theirs. And in the process of being rewarded with a driver's license, my sons now also hold the life-long honor that comes with being an Eagle.

That hard-earned "piece of plastic" bears a lot of responsibility—the ability to make possible life and death decisions. It is important for your children to understand the responsibility they are taking on along with the increased freedom and "coolness." Have your kids spend a year volunteering at a nearby hospital, where they will undoubtedly see the cost of reckless driving.

ACT NOW

Date _____

Before the sun goes down, think of something your child has asked for recently (I'm sure you've got several to choose from), and create a meaningful task she can complete to earn it. Have the discussion about why you're going to do this from now on, and then vow to be the cheerleader, scorekeeper...and the one who rewards.

_____
Signature

My child wants _____

_____

He/she can earn it by_____

_____

MORE HELP

There are many great sites on the internet full of tips on how to effectively link the concept of hard work with just reward.

- LifeScript.com and helium.com have a collection of articles on creating effective and engaging tasks for children, including articles such as "10 Tips on How to Make a Chore List for Children."

- Kidsoffthecouch.com offers a great weekly email blast of ideas on how to do just that—a great source to draw from when looking for meaningful tasks for your children.

One of my favorite writers on the topic of instilling good work ethic is Dr. Eileen Gallo. She, along with her husband Jon coauthored *The Financially Intelligent Parent: 8 Steps to Raising Successful, Generous, Responsible Children*. They are also the authors of the critically-acclaimed book *Silver Spoon Kids: How Successful Parents Raise Responsible Children*. They are the principals of The Gallo Institute, a national organization offering education and counsel to families and financial advisors on the issues of families, children and money.

CLUBMOM.com is also an excellent online community and forum where you can find successful tips from other parents and experts on different ways to teach kids the value of hard work.

Teach Your Children
To Be Good Stewards

THE CHALLENGE

Ask ten young people to define capitalism. Chances are that most will talk about it in context of materialism and greed.

Today's teens have been the pupils of a generation that has created America's worst economic crises in several decades. In general, Americans spend more than they earn and rely too heavily on credit cards and loans. Most are not saving enough (if anything) for their futures. And, when they get in financial trouble, there is a growing mentality that the government will take care of them.

It's no wonder that young people confuse capitalism with consumerism, devaluing the principles of saving, thrift, personal responsibility, and charity. Capitalism, when properly applied, creates a situation where everybody wins—consumers, suppliers, businesses, and the overall economy. But capitalism practiced in a vacuum of morality creates greed and fosters an environment where people and their money are squandered and where corruption breeds.

When referring to the passing of wealth and financial skills within families, sociologists often refer to the cycle of "shirtsleeves to shirtsleeves in three generations." BBC News reports that this old American saying originated in the late 1800s when there was booming wealth in the United States. The wealthy class "handed [their] money on as a life belt to their sons who then squandered it, so much so that their sons returned to the shirtsleeves in which [their] grandfather had landed in the United States."

In other words, the cycle of wealth and work would begin with someone toiling to build a fortune from almost nothing. They then, wanting to spare their own children the pain of hard work, and to give their children the privileges they never had, spoil them rotten. Those children grow up with little-to-no understanding of work ethic, squander their fortune, and leave nothing for their own children. Those children, disgusted with their own parents, reject the life of laziness and greed, and begin rebuilding.

This may be an exaggerated version of what we see today, but it is undeniable that it is critical we teach our children to be good stewards of their money, their talents, and their futures. Parents who spoil their children and do not teach them about the value of money and property will raise them to be greedy and confused. It is only a matter of time before they destroy themselves, whether it's in home debt, credit card bills, gambling, or some other financial irresponsibility.

Statistics paint a dismal picture:

- Only 27 percent of parents surveyed in 2003 by Fleet Boston felt well-informed about managing household finances.

- Fewer than half of those surveyed felt they are good role models for their children regarding saving and spending.
- In 2004, the average credit card debt among 25 to 35-year-olds, including parents, was $5,200—nearly twice as many as in 1992.

Yet:

- 94 percent of students say their parents are their primary teachers on financial matters.
- 79 percent of high school students have never taken a course on personal finance.

It's no wonder that:

- 82 percent of teens failed a basic quiz evaluating their knowledge of financial management.
- The average college student graduates with $27,600 of debt.

If we want to help secure our children's financial future, a good first step is teaching our children how to handle their money, rather than allowing their money to handle them. Helping them understand how to be wise stewards is a gift that can free them from the emptiness that comes with materialism, the disparity that comes with debt, the joy that comes with financial stability, and the fulfillment that comes with philanthropy. When it comes down to it, the overall solution is actually very simple—live within your means, save and plan for the future, and be generous to others. Imagine what our children's future would be if they, as a generation, started practicing these basic principles?

Fortunately, there is a "wealth" of sound advice on the issues of money that you and your kids can "bank on." The Bible addresses economic issues with surprising frequency. As a matter of fact, as Crown Financial Ministries points out, there are 2,350 verses in the Bible on money and stewardship, making it "second to the subject of love as the most discussed subject in the Bible. In fact, two-thirds of the parables that Jesus taught are about money, possessions, and stewardship." Regardless of your denomination or faith, the wisdom of this all-time best-seller is undeniable—and incredibly applicable to our world today. Here are just a few examples:

- "Where your treasure is, there will your heart be also." (Matthew 6:21 and Luke 12:34)
- "The wise man saves for the future, but the foolish man spends whatever he gets." (Proverbs 21:20)
- "The wicked borrow and never repay but the godly are generous givers," (Psalm 37:21)
- "The rich rules over the poor, and the borrower becomes the lender's slave." (Proverbs 22:7).
- "A good man leaves an inheritance to his children's children." (Proverbs 13:22).
- "Steady plodding brings prosperity." (Proverbs 21:5).

One of the most telling verses is from I Timothy 6:10: "For the love of money is the root of all evil: which while some coveted after, they have erred from the faith, and have pierced themselves through with many sorrows." Notice how it says the *love of* money is the root of evil—not money itself. And how true it is that those who covet money injure themselves with sorrow! If you've ever felt the burden of financial trouble, you know just how deeply it can impact your very soul and outlook on life. Don't we want to do everything we can to spare our children from such sorrow?

Some of the greatest Americans have also had a thing or two to say about the importance of good financial principles. Benjamin Franklin coined the famous phrase, "A penny saved is a penny earned" and others, such as "Buy what thou hast no need of, and e'er long thou shalt sell thy necessaries" and "He that goes a-borrowing goes a-sorrowing."

"One should be a civilized man, saving something, and not a savage, consuming every day all that which he has earned," steel magnate Andrew Carnegie writes in his book *The Empire of Business.* According to him, thrift was the "first duty" of those who aspire to wealth.

We should help our children memorize these wise sayings, and offer them ongoing practical ways to implement the principles they embody.

IN YOUR SHOES

Claudia responded to one of my columns and shared her story about teaching her son financial responsibility:

Even as a very small child, our son, Thomas, tuned in to fashion trends. He wasn't interested in fads or what they were wearing on T.V. because we didn't watch T.V. As a Kindergartener, he decided his Easter Sunday wardrobe before we even talked about shopping. He wanted to wear a white shirt, grey slacks, and a red bow tie. I never knew how he made thatdecision; perhaps from something he saw in print. We were happy to comply with his request and he looked great that Easter. As he grew older, his fashion sense grew ever stronger. As a stay at home mother, it became much harder to find a compromise on costly items. Thomas didn't demand outrageous, inappropriate items, but what appealed to him became increasingly expensive. His interest in designer brands threatened our tight budget. After struggling with the issue, my husband and I came up with asolution that worked for all of us. Before we went shopping, we set a dollar amount that we could afford to spend for each item. If Thomas wished to make a purchase exceeding that limit he would be required to make up the difference from his own funds (allowance, odd jobs, birthdayor Christmas gift money.) This idea worked extremely well. Even though still quite young, Thomas became acutely aware of expenses. He would do his homework and watch the ads, shopping for sale items. He learned to watch prices and makewise decisions in other areas as well. We didn't know it at the time,but we were raising a Financial Analyst. Now he is 27 years old, works for a great Fortune 500 firm and is on schedule to complete his MBA next spring. Oh—and he always looks great!

Carol wrote to me about how she keeps financial lessons and rules simple and linked to everyday actions in her child's life:

There are only two rules:

1. They have to earn their allowance with a specific set of household chores. If they slack off the chores, I dock their allowance. Bonuses and incentives are allowed if they do something remarkable, i.e., waxing the car rather than just washing it.

2. Allowance is paid weekly, in cash. They get the allowance on Sunday, before they go to church, and have been encouraged to share in the offering that morning. If they spend all the money by 5:00 p.m. on Monday, they are out of money for the rest of the week. When they've come to me on Wednesday asking for an advance on next week's allowance I've only had to say once or twice, 'No, because I can't get an advance on my salary.'

Teach Your Children To Be Good Stewards

The only exception is if there is something really big that they want that they can use to actually earn more money (like a lawn mower they can use to start a business or a bicycle to get to their job, etc.). Loan them the money, have them sign a note for it, and work out a reasonable payment schedule that leaves them something to spend.

And here's one of my own personal stories:

When my son was entering his pre-teen years, fashion suddenly became more important to him. He wanted to go shopping for new clothes, so I decided it would be a great opportunity to teach him the importance of thrift. We went to a department store and selected new shirts and pants. We bought three non-designer shirts at a pretty hefty price tag. We then drove down the street to a Goodwill outlet that I knew was very clean, organized, and stocked full of used clothing in great condition. I let Drew go through the rows and rows of clothes and pick out as many shirts as he wanted. Boy, did he find a huge selection! We then added up the price of the shirts and I said, 'Now, you can have the three shirts we bought at Hecht's, or you can have all nine of these and keep the difference.' A sparkle flashed across Drew's eyes as he realized the obvious choice—it was clear to me that he also discovered the value of thrift that day. Drew is now in his early twenties, and he always goes to thrift and consignment stores first when he needs or wants new clothes. It has been a fabulous lesson that is not only good for his personal finances, but it also shows how much waste there is. Our teen daughter, Kristin, enjoys the treasure hunt of looking for dresses at consignment stores. Nick, who is in college, enjoys looking for unusual jackets and unique T-shirts. We aren't always successful in such trips and do often end up in the mall. But it is a blessing to me to see the joy and satisfaction on their faces each time they find something they love—and how much we didn't spend. It actually makes them feel good for not slamming my bank account, and there is always a sense of appreciation and sense of accomplishment on both sides—for me and them.

ACT NOW

Date _____

Today I ordered a workbook or course on responsible finance for kids/teens (and one for me, too!).

_____
Signature

Teach Your Children To Be Good Stewards

■ In 2004, my husband and I took a class on money management that changed our lives. Our church was offering the Crown Financial Ministries course that focuses on the moral underpinnings, basic principles and practical tools of finances. Crown is, "an interdenominational ministry dedicated to equipping people around the world to learn, apply, and teach biblical financial principles. Crown has taught or equipped more than 50 million people in over 40 nations with the life-transforming message of faithfully living by God's financial principles in every area of their lives. The ministry is located in the United States, Canada, Latin America, South America, and Africa, and is expanding into Europe, India, Asia, and Australia." Given that hundreds of churches around the country offer Crown courses, you just might find one near you. Check out their website, crown.org, for locations. Even if they don't have a class in your neighborhood, you will find just about everything you need to help you get your own financial house in order and teach your children how to build theirs. The site features interactive exercises, daily tips, devotionals, and personal study on finances. They even offer the services of a personal financial coach! And their newsletter on "Life and Financial Coaching" will encourage, bless, and equip you on a regular basis. Crown also has a 10-week study guide for teens, *Discovering God's Way of Handling Money Teen Study,* that "is designed to practically help teens create habits that will set them on a lifelong journey of handling money responsibly." If Crown were the only financial resource in the world, you would have everything you need to teach you and your kids how to live well.

■ Focus on the Family also offers articles and books devoted to strengthening the family through teaching sound money understanding for children of all age levels. You can access wonderful resources at family.org

continued

- 279 -

MORE HELP

where they provide links to great materials created by numerous financial advisors and experts—all holding the worldview that we should be secure in our own finances so that we can help others and share God's love most fully.

■ Money Smart World (moneysmartworld.com), a secular organization based in the United Kingdom is definitely worth your time. As the organization states: "Our aim is to provide resources that make it easier for parents and teachers to teach children about money and to help them develop money management skills and financial habits that will last a lifetime." They offer free worksheets and reasonably priced interactive workbooks for parents to work through with children of all ages. Their teen program, states, "Although this may be one of the most challenging times to teach your teens about money, it is very important for them to realise that their behaviour, and the decisions taken at this stage really has consequences. The skills they need to master include the ability to "earn money, commit to saving goals, plan and budget, spend wisely, understand philanthropy and how to connect money and the future."

■ And then there is the great Dave Ramsey—noted author, speaker, radio host and "all around" genius on finances. Dave has a fabulous website chock full of great tips at daveramsey.com. He also offers one of the most fantastic, life-changes programs for teens I've ever seen—*Generation Change*. Dave created this program because, "Every day, our youth are bombarded with a million different voices—everything from billboards to internet ads—telling them who they are and measuring their worth by what they have. The pressure to be accepted in today's stuff-centered world drives them, and perhaps even their parents, to

continued

MORE HELP

throw money away on things that don't matter—all in an attempt to 'be somebody.' The result? We're raising a generation that spends money they don't have to buy things they don't need to impress people they don't even like! It's time for a change!" The course is taught by video and comes with a Leader's Guide.

Now for a bit of parting general advice: Don't overwhelm your child by trying to teach him or her everything there is to know about money at once. Start with simple principles and digestible points.

Make Your Own List

THE CHALLENGE

As I've stated before, kids don't come from cookie cutters. And neither do families! So although this book contains 30 specific steps to
take in order to protect yours, it probably doesn't contain all the issues
that might be of particular concern to you. My goal was to start you
on the path to realizing that there are concrete steps you can take that
actually work, and to get you to take them—one at a time. But I obviously didn't have the room to cover everything. There's probably a
little list already going in your head of other subjects you need help
with.

Every family is going to have unique challenges and "opportunities," as I like to call them. You may have even been tempted to ignore

some of the most difficult problem areas and opportunities in your family, maybe because you feel alone or as if you'll never be able to solve them.

Don't give up! Hopefully, this book has shown you that you can find help for just about every problem you may encounter. Here are the steps to take in coming up with your own list.

- ❏ **Identify the THE CHALLENGE** (Each of my chapters start by doing this.) Writing out the problem will help you focus on just what it is that is bothering you. Think about the harms the problem can cause, and any specific facts that back up why you think there is a problem in the first place.

- ❏ **Identify the solution.** What is the general obvious solution to the problem at hand? The general solution isn't usually rocket science, as I have said. But the solution may contain many steps that need to be taken over a long period of time. That's ok. You will be encouraged to know that there is a definitive solution that could be available to you. Doing this section should bring you hope. After all, if you have a problem and know that a solution exists, you can start working toward it! The difficult part is usually coming up with one concrete step you can take to begin solving the problem.

- ❏ **Identify the action.** What is the one concrete action you can take TODAY to help you on your way? Don't make it hard or complicated. You are far better off taking baby steps at first. Just make sure you can do what you write down—even writing it down is part of the action.

- ❏ **Repeat step #3.** As you have read in this book, some problems can actually be solved quite easily—like ending the threat that online pornography poses to your children by getting a reliable internet filter. (But even on that one-step problem-solver, you do have to follow-up to make sure it is still working, that your kids haven't hacked into it, etc.) Other problems need the action repeated several times. One example is the section on becoming your family's movie critic. You can't just do it once—you need to find a useful tool that will help identify harmful and wholesome films each time your child wants to go to the movies. So, think about whether or not the action you listed needs to be repeated. If so, word your action that way so you are reminded to that it is an ongoing process.

❏ **Talk to others to find out what worked for them.** I included personal stories in many chapters to let you know that others have gone before you! On the vast majority of issues parents face, there is another parent somewhere that has had to bear that burden before you. Seek out the wisest people you know and ask them for their success stories.

FROM MY HOME TO YOURS

As you well know by now, I have used many tips from others throughout this book. We can all benefit from the experiences of others to save our families. I wanted you to have plenty of information on each subject so I have supplied a list of resources in the back of this book. Those have come from others, too—special thanks to Becky Norton Dunlop, Bridgett Wagner, and Colin Sharkey for help in compiling a list of organizations.

Although many of the stories from readers of my weekly column made it into a chapter or two, most did not. In closing, I thought it might be helpful to provide a list of tips from readers that aren't included elsewhere. Perhaps some of these relate to the list you are making.

IN YOUR SHOES

The following are from a reader named Galen:

1. My wife and I are totally committed to each other and we stand as a parental unit. Yes, there are times we disagree and sometimes don't even "like" one another, but we are committed and love each other even when we don't feel like it.

2. Children must be accountable and responsible for their conduct. They also have to be allowed to make mistakes, so long as they will not "crush" them physically, emotionally or spiritually. That's when parenting takes over. They have to be allowed to make decisions and choices and live with the consequences. As the decision process becomes better, more liberty and leeway has to be given.

3. Education is important. It is their job while they are at home. Work, recreation, etc. is dictated by whether or not their studies are done. When grades fall, so do privileges.

4. Where we will be on Sunday morning is not open to debate; we will be in God's house. The rest of the week, God will be in our house.

5. Hang onto the scripture that says "bring up a child in the way he should go and when he is old he will not stray from it."

John wrote:

1) I am a financial advisor. I have brought several books home for my children to read, books that I give to my clients. I started doing that over ten years ago, and I continue to do that today. My children will not grow as financially illiterate as I was at their age.

2) My wife and I support our children's efforts even if we don't agree with them. We do, however, reserve the right to veto any activity in our home, and we have done so. When we do veto an activity, we always explain why. Usually, a simple sentence will do, given the background we have established. For example, I have vetoed Instant Messaging on the family computer for two reasons, one being the use of the bandwidth of our Internet connection and the other being the exposure of our private information. The girls knew that I was not going to give in on this, so there was no argument.

Carol limits the use of video games for her twelve-year-old son, and shared what she provides for him instead:

That something has turned out to be adventure stories written for boys on CD. Like most twelve-year-old boys, our son struggles with reading for long lengths of time. He is dyslexic, and it is physically hard for him to concentrate on the written word for more than about twenty minutes. But he's more than happy to listen to someone else read. So where we skip spending money on video games, we use the money to buy him books written by G. A. Henty on CD, or a series like The Hobbit or Lord of the Rings (unabridged), and I found some excellent stores of famous naval battles, WWII battles, and military weaponry through the ages.

Michael offered many wonderful ideas that he had successfully used in his own home, including this helpful list of milestones:

Growing up, our children had milestones they could anticipate and prepare for.

Age eight they could have friends sleep over, with parental consent.

Age ten they got their Military Dependent ID card and a later bed time.

Age twelve they could get their ears pieced, including our son. (He did not get them pierced). And a later bed time.—Age fourteen, they were allowed to wear some make-up. And a later bed time.

Age fifteen, Dad and Mom taught them to drive a car and they got their permit. They were allowed to go to school dances. And they were allowed to get a job as long as they kept their grades as A's and B's.

Age sixteen, they were allowed to date; first two dates to be at our house or their date's house. And a vehicle would be available for them to drive when they had their license. They had a curfew; the city curfew was 11:00 PM and that was theirs as well. We treated them as adults and encouraged them to think and act as such.

Age seventeen they set their own curfew, as long as it was reasonable. They had to cover their own expenses for the automobile.

For graduating High School they got a good, used, vehicle.—Age eighteen we took them to register to vote, and we started charging them rent.

Age twenty-five, they will get all the rent money back.

Michael also said:

We taught them to give God the first fruits of their labor, a 10 percent tithe. We taught them to then save 20 percent of their earnings for "retirement," and to save another 10 to 20 percent for car repairs and other emergencies. They do this to this day.

We taught them that school was their primary job and they had to do their best in all areas. As well, they had chores at home in order to learn responsibility, and an allowance which they earned by doing them.

My wife of 25 years and I taught our children that marriage is to the death. It hasn't all been sunshine and peaches, but most of it was, and still is. Respect for each other has gone a long way toward our happiness. I think we imparted that to our children.

Carolyn described how her family marched to the beat of their own drummer:

I did things pretty much in reverse of what was considered the norm. My only child was born when I was thirty-three. I continued to practice law until he was five years old and ready to start school, at which time, I closed up shop and went home to raise my child. We home schooled for two years in a neighborhood where most of the children were home schooled. It was a wonderful time, and the children thrived. There were field trips with formal home school groups for science experiments, lessons of all kinds, as well as just for fun.

Then we moved to the country. We slowly acquired goats, donkeys, chickens, cows, turkeys...and the list goes on. For several years, I home schooled another child the same age as my son. We did every subject every day, and were finished by noon. There was no nonsense in the classroom. Although it was relaxed and fun, the kids knew they were there to learn. In the afternoons, they were free to be little boys, building forts in the field, helping with the animals, riding their bikes, *or whatever they wanted to do. It was a wonderful time, and the kids were terrific.*

Jane described a program her school put together for parents:

At our school, the parents would get together at the beginning of the year and after an introduction, broke into groups of 6-8 to compare notes on curfew times, what entertainment was allowed in their homes, and limits parents put on their kids' behaviors. Lo and behold the parents found out that other kids had strict and earlier curfews, and much more restrictive controls than their kids had reported. Kids had told their parents that say, Timmy or Abdul, could stay out until eleven on weeknights, when Timmy's/Abdul's parents had a strict eight PM limit on weeknights/eleven PM weekends, and no midnight movies, since nothing good happens after midnight. Right away, parents were empowered and encouraged to set and enforce limits for their kids. A police officer was brought in another time to show parents innocent-looking rave paraphernalia (pacifiers, funny candy) they might not be familiar with, and stats for accidents while driving with friends were also discussed. Perhaps the strictest warning to parents was that if they served their kids and others alcohol— even at a private party—they would be charged for underage drinking. Another theme before Christmas, so it was early, was to NOT allow kids to go on Spring Break trips. News reports were shown of kids, drunk out of their minds, jumping to their deaths because of their altered state.

And, here is my final tip for keeping your child safe that didn't fit neatly into one chapter, but is something you should do TODAY:

Make Your Own List

Know where the sex offenders are in your area. Convicted sex offenders are required by law to register with the government and include their current addresses. With just a few clicks you can find out if there are any living in your neighborhood or near your child's school. Just go to justice.org and click on the Sex Offender Website. The website is free and compiled by The United States Justice Department. It provides detailed information on registered sex offenders (for example, those who have already been caught, convicted, and released back into the public—in other words, only those we know about) and enter your zip codes. The results will likely disturb you: you'll see the names and faces of all the sex convicts who live in your town—and in your own neighborhood. The numbers are absolutely stunning. But don't stop there. Put your children and teens in the car and drive by the houses where these convicted child molesters live—and tell your kids to stay away. I've done it every time we have moved homes since the service became available.

ACT NOW

Date _____

Today I began making my own list of family problems and began writing down the solutions and actions I can take to help solve them.

_____
Signature

MORE HELP

CONCERNED FAMILIES
(FATHERS, MOTHERS, AND YOUTH) (concernedfamilies.org)

- Concerned Fathers Against Crime conduct neighborhood watch programs in conjunction with law enforcement to help keep communities safe.

- Concerned Mothers Alliance for Children write letters to express concern about the increasingly negative culture and its affect on children.

- Concerned Youth brings children and adults together to serve their communities.

Even More Help

*Compiled in this guide are some additional great resources,
along with some of the ones I mentioned in the book
listed here for your convenience.*

ABSTINENCE CLEARINGHOUSE
801 East 41st Street
Sioux Falls, SD 57105
605-335-3643
abstinence.net
The Abstinence Clearinghouse is a non-profit educational organization
that promotes the practice of sexual abstinence through distribution of
various factual and medically-accurate materials. The Clearinghouse
helps strengthen national, state, local, and international agencies through
various services and provides a central location where character, relationship and abstinence programs, curricula, speakers, and materials
could be accessed.

ALLIANCE DEFENSE FUND

15333 North Pima Road, Suite 165

Scottsdale, AZ   85260

480-444-0020

telladf.org

The Alliance Defense Fund was founded to aggressively defend religious liberty by empowering our allies and working to assist them in their efforts through strategy, training, funding, and, where necessary, direct litigation through our own ADF legal team.

AMERICAN CENTER FOR LAW AND JUSTICE

201 Maryland Avenue, NE

Washington, DC 20002

202-546-8890

aclj.org

The American Center for Law and Justice is a not-for-profit public interest law firm and educational organization dedicated to the promotion of pro-liberty, pro-life, and pro-family causes.

AMERICAN FAMILY ASSOCIATION

P. O. Drawer 2440

Tupelo, MS 38803

662-844-5036

afa.net

The American Family Association represents and stands for traditional values, focusing primarily on the influence of television and other media—including pornography—on our society.

ASKLISTENLEARN.COM

The Century Council, an organization dedicated to fighting drunk driving and underaged drinking and Nickelodeon have created a guide for kids on responsible decision-making regarding alcohol and how to say no.

BSAFE ONLINE
P.O. Box 1819
Bristol, TN 37620
850-362-4310
bsafe.com
Bsafe Online is dedicated to keeping children, families, and small businesses safe while using the Internet.

BOY SCOUTS OF AMERICA, NATIONAL COUNCIL
(NATIONAL CAPITAL AREA COUNCIL)
9190 Rockville Pike
Bethesda, MD   20814-3897
301-530-9360
scouting.org
The mission of the Boy Scouts of America is to prepare young people to make ethical and moral choices over their lifetimes by instilling in them the values of the Scout Oath and Law.

CAFEMOM.COM
CafeMom features include fully customizable profile pages, friends' networks, journaling, a widget platform and strong privacy / anonymity controls. CafeMom is focused on creating a great site for moms that is somewhere they can come to get advice, feel supported, make friends or just relax.

CAMPAIGN FOR A COMMERCIAL-FREE CHILDHOOD
53 Parker Hill Ave.
Boston, MA 02120
617-278-4172
CCFC's mission is to reclaim childhood from corporate marketers

CITIZENS FOR COMMUNITY VALUES
11175 Reading Road, Suite 103
Cincinnati, OH 45241
513-733-5775
ccv.org
CCV is a grassroots organization of citizens who are concerned for the well-being of the community, the strength of its families, and the future of its children.

CONCERNED FAMILIES (FATHERS, MOTHERS, AND YOUTH)
233 Rogue River Hwy
Grants Pass, OR 97527
concernedfamilies.org
This unique three-tier organization has developed a simple system based on the principle that the traditional family is a transforming power, and thus a "community family" can also be transforming.

CONCERNED WOMEN FOR AMERICA
1015 15th Street, NW, Suite 1100
Washington, DC 20005
202-488-7000
cwfa.org
The mission of CWA is to protect and promote Biblical values among all citizens—first through prayer, then education, and finally by influencing our society—thereby reversing the decline in moral values in our nation.

CONTROLYOURTV.COM
controlyourtv.org
The site features information on cable's blocking technology, descriptions of family-friendly cable programming, and resources devoted to media literacy and education.

CROWN FINANCIAL MINISTRIES
P.O. Box 100
Gainesville, GA 30503-0100
800-722-1976
crown.org
Equipping people worldwide to learn, apply, and teach God's financial principles so they may know Christ more intimately, be free to serve Him, and help fund the Great Commission.

EMILY POST INSTITUTE
444 South Union Street
Burlington, VT 05401
emilypost.com
The Emily Post Institute, created by Emily in 1946 and run today by third generation family members, serves as a "civility barometer" for American society and continues Emily's work. That work has grown to address the societal concerns of the 21st century including business etiquette, raising polite children and civility in America.

DAVE RAMSEY
888-TALK-BAK
daveramsey.com
Dave Ramsey offers life-changing financial advice as host of the nationally syndicated radio program, The Dave Ramsey Show, heard by nearly 3 million listeners each week on more than 375 radio stations throughout the United States.

ENOUGH IS ENOUGH
746 Walker Road, Suite 116
Great Falls, VA 22066
enough.org
"Make the internet Safer for children and families."

FAMILY BIBLE LIBRARY
2451 Atrium Way
Nashville, TN 37214
1-888-551-5901
southwesternfamilyresources.com
Provides Christian-based educational products for families.

FAMILY ENTERTAINMENT CENTRAL
535 East Fulton, Suite 1A
Grand Rapids, MI 49503
familyentertainmentcentral.org
The Family Entertainment Association provides easy access to in-depth information for current entertainment media including movies, DVDs, electronic games, television, and music.

FAMILYFACTS.COM
214 Massachusetts Avenue NE
Washington DC 20002
The Heritage Foundation's familyfacts.org catalogs social science findings on the family, society and religion gleaned from peer-reviewed journals, books and government surveys.

FAMILYLIFE
P.O. Box 7111
Little Rock, AR 72223
1-800-FL-TODAY
familylife.com
Family Life's mission is to effectively develop godly marriages and families and help them change the world one home at a time.

FAMILYTIME.COM
43 North Avenue
Bridgeport, CT 06606
FamilyTime provides you with online household organization, menu planning, and money-saving applications, as well as advice from home organization and cooking experts on how you can best run your household.

FAMILIESWITHPURPOSE.COM
5690 Whitfield
Troy, MI 48098
888-210-8958
"We inspire and enable parents to create a meaningful family life for themselves and their children by providing products, resources, and services which empower parents to take control of their family life and build a warm and loving home."

FOCUS ON THE FAMILY
8605 Explorer Drive
Colorado Springs, CO 80920
719-268-4811
fotf.org
Focus on the Family's mission is to cooperate with the Holy Spirit in sharing the Gospel of Jesus Christ with as many people as possible by nurturing and defending the God-ordained institution of the family and promoting biblical truths worldwide.

thetruthproject.org
The Truth Project is a DVD-based small group curriculum comprised of 12 one-hour lessons taught by Dr. Del Tackett. This home study is the starting point for looking at life from a biblical perspective.

HAPPY HOUSEWIVES CLUB
happyhousewivesclub.com
Created by Darla Shine, this website is an invaluable resource for every stay-at-home mom. From mealtimes to fitness, there's advice and tips on everything today's housewife needs to know when raising her kids.

HOME SCHOOL LEGAL DEFENSE ASSOCIATION
P.O. Box 3000

Purcellville, VA 20134

540-338-5600

hslda.org/federal

Home School Legal Defense Association is a nonprofit advocacy organization established to defend and advance the constitutional right of parents to direct the education of their children and to protect family freedoms.

INTERNET SOLUTIONS FOR KIDS
1820 E. Garry Ave. Suite 105

Santa Ana, CA 92705

Is4k.com

Our mission is to promote new and innovative methods that improve the health and safety of young people.

KIDSOFFTHECOUCH.COM
Kids Off the Couch is a free, weekly e-mail that provides families with fresh ideas for getting kids off the couch and into their city.

MODEST BY DESIGN
888-756-0944

modestbydesign.com

We at Modest by Design believe that dressing modestly shows respect not only for ones self but for God and his commandments. We also believe that we can set an example for the world that it is possible to dress modestly as well as fashionably.

MONEYSMARTWORLD.COM
The MoneySmart workbooks have been designed as a tool for improving financial literacy amongst kids and teenagers by helping them start good financial habits that will last a lifetime.

Even More Help

MOVIEGUIDE
1-800-577-6684
movieguide.org
A monthly magazine that helps parents gain a better understanding of the content of specific movies by rating the overall "moral acceptability" of the movie and covering what type of objectionable material the film may have along with the moral context in which these are deployed.

NATIONAL CABLE AND TELECOMMUNICATION ASSOCIATION
25 Massachusetts Avenue, NW
Suite 100
Washington, DC 20001-1413
Phone: (202) 222-2300
Founded in 1952, NCTA's primary mission is to provide its members with a strong national presence by providing a single, unified voice on issues affecting the cable and telecommunications industry.

NATIONAL INSTITUTE ON MEDIA AND THE FAMILY
606 24th Avenue South, Suite 606
Minneapolis, MN 55454
612-672-5437
Since 1996, the National Institute on Media and the Family has worked tirelessly to help parents and communities "watch what our kids watch.".

NATIONAL ORGANIZATION FOR MARRIAGE
20 Nassau Street, Suite 242
Princeton, NJ 8542
609-688-0450
nationformarriage.org
The National Organization for Marriage (NOM) is a nonprofit organization with a mission to protect marriage and the faith communities that sustain it. Founded in response to the growing need for an organized opposition to same-sex marriage in state legislatures, NOM serves as a national resource for marriage-related initiatives at the state and local level.

PARENTS TELEVISION COUNCIL
707 Wilshire Boulevard #2075
Los Angeles, CA 90017
800-882-6868
parentstv.org
Bringing America's demand for positive, family oriented television programming to the entertainment industry.

PASSING THE BATON
passingthebaton.org
At this site, you can join others in receiving in-depth training on how to influence not only your kids, but their entire generation to be the next great leaders.

PLUGGEDINONLINE.COM
Plugged In, Focus on the Family
Colorado Springs, CO 80995
800-A-FAMILY
pluggedinonline.com
A website offering reviews of a wide variety of movies, music and television shows to help parents make a more informed decision about what their children can see and hear.

PROMISE KEEPERS
P.O. Box 11798
Denver, CO 80211-0798
866-PROMISE
promisekeepers.org
Promise Keepers is dedicated to igniting and uniting men to be passionate followers of Jesus Christ through the effective communication of the 7 Promises.

SALVO MAGAZINE
P.O. Box 410788
Chicago, IL 60641
773-481-1090
salvomag.com
"Recovering the one worldview that actually works. "

SUMMIT MINISTRIES
summit.org
866-786-6483
Summit Ministries tries to counteract the negative ideas of the modern world by training youth to stand strong in their faith.

THE DOVE FOUNDATION
535 East Fulton, Suite 1A
Grand Rapids, MI 49503
866-WEB-WISE
dove.org
The mission of the Dove Foundation is to encourage and promote the creation, production, distribution and consumption of wholesome family entertainment.

THE NATIONAL CAMPAIGN TO PREVENT TEEN PREGNANCY
1776 Massachusetts Avenue, NW, Suite 200
Washington, DC 20036
202-478-8500
thenationalcampaign.org
The National Campaign seeks to improve the well-being of children, youth, families, and the nation by preventing unplanned and teen pregnancy.

THE NATIONAL LAW CENTER FOR CHILDREN AND FAMILIES
225 North Fairfax Street
Alexandria, VA 22314
703-548-5522
nationallawcenter.org
The National Law Center is a not-for-profit organization whose mission is the protection of children and families from the harmful effect of illegal pornography by assisting in law enforcement and law improvement.

THE RUTHERFORD INSTITUTE
P.O. Box 7482
Charlottesville, VA 22906
434-978-3888
The Rutherford Institute is an organization dedicated to the defense of civil liberties and human rights.

TWENTIETH CENTURY FOX
Twentieth Century Fox has joined with the Dove Foundation in the effort to produce and promote quality family entertainment. Family-approved films will be marked with Dove's "seal of approval," making shielding the family easier to do.

UNITED STATES JUSTICE FOUNDATION
932 D Street, Suite 2
Ramona, CA 92065
760-788-6624
usjf.net
The United States Justice Foundation is a nonprofit public interest, legal action organization dedicated to instruct, inform and educate the public on, and to litigate, significant legal issues confronting America.

Even More Help

VISION FORUM MINISTRIES
4719 Blanco Road
San Antonio, TX 78212
visionforumministries.org
"Preserving Our Covenant with God through Biblical Patriarchy and Multi-Generational Faithfulness."

WEB WISE KIDS
P.O. Box 27203
Santa Ana, CA 92799
webwisekids.org
Webwise kids help ensure child Internet safety by giving tips and advice to parents and children on how to protect themselves from online predators.

WOMEN OF FAITH
womenoffaith.com
Women of Faith is a faith-based women's organization encouraging women of all ages and stages in life to grow in faith and spiritual maturity through a relationship with Jesus Christ and an understanding of God's love and grace.

WORLDVIEW ACADEMY
800-241-1123
Worldview Academy trains students and adults to understand their faith as a total worldview. They offer resources to help families continue to grow.

YOUNG AMERICA'S FOUNDATION
110 Elden Street
Herndon, VA 20170
703-318-9608
yaf.org
Young America's Foundation is committed to ensuring that increasing numbers of young Americans understand and are inspired by the ideas of individual freedom, a strong national defense, free enterprise, and traditional values.

YOUNG LIFE
P.O. Box 520
Colorado Springs, CO 80901
877-438-9572
younglife.org
Young life's mission is to introduce adolescents to Jesus Christ and help them grow in their faith by building relationships.

Index

Index

Index

Index